PIZZAS AND P

An exciting range of recipes and
sandwich syndrome and provide varied and wholesome meals
in an economic way.

By the same author

A VEGETARIAN IN THE FAMILY
THE RAW FOOD WAY TO HEALTH
THE WHOLEFOOD LUNCH BOX
THE WHOLEFOOD SWEETS BOOK
QUICHES AND FLANS
PASTA DISHES
SIMPLE AND SPEEDY WHOLEFOOD COOKING

PIZZAS AND PANCAKES

by

JANET HUNT

Illustrated by Clive Birch

THORSONS PUBLISHERS LIMITED
Wellingborough, Northamptonshire

First published May 1982
Second Impression October 1982

British Library Cataloguing in Publication Data

Hunt, Janet
    Pizzas and pancakes.
    1. Vegetarian cookery
    2. Pancakes, waffles, etc.   3. Pizza
    I. Title
    641.5'636   TX837

    ISBN 0-7225-0723-2

Typeset by Glebe Graphics, Wilby, Northamptonshire.
Printed and bound in Great Britain by
Richard Clay (The Chaucer Press) Ltd.,
Bungay, Suffolk.

CONTENTS

Wholefoods, quite simply, are foods in their natural state – nothing added, nothing taken away. In this age of mass-production foods, wholefoods are not always easy to obtain. But as nutritionalists and doctors become increasingly convinced, of their value in building and maintaining health, so their availability is fast improving.

Include as many natural, unadulterated foods as you can in your day to day eating pattern, and discover not just exciting new tastes and a fresh approach to mealtimes, but better health too.

PIZZAS TO PLEASE

It was not so long ago that if you wanted to eat pizza you had to go to Italy. Limited food supplies, particularly in the poverty-stricken South, had to be stretched to feed large families, and the pizza was one of the dishes that resulted from this need. A tasty combination of dough base (often stale bread!) and vegetable topping, with a tiny amount of cheese, fish or meat, it offered carbohydrate and protein and was as filling as it was inexpensive.

In recent years, however, pizza has become one of the world's most popular fast-foods. You can now enjoy it in elegant restaurants, corner cafés and canteens. Pubs serve it with a pint. Supermarkets offer do-it-yourself kits as well as the frozen variety. And take-away pizza parlours are everywhere. Pizzas can be a meal or a snack; can be enjoyed hot or cold; eaten with knife and fork, or served in slices to be held in the hand and munched like a sandwich. And those who haven't eaten it one way or another are rare – it really does seem to appeal to everyone.

The fact that pizzas are so readily available is probably one of the reasons so few people make their own. Another one may be that the traditional dough is made from yeast, and so takes a little more effort and time than many other home-made dishes. In fact, pizzas can be made without too much trouble. And for the 'wholefooder' they offer a perfect solution to the family with the big appetite and the small budget, as well as being a sneaky but highly successful way to get children who prefer junk foods to eat healthily –and enjoy it. When eating pizza out, the variety of toppings is usually rather limited, and the resulting dish nowhere near as nutritious as it could be, (unless, of course, you are eating at a wholefood restaurant). Make your pizza at home and you can make it a real 'health' food.

Substitute a crunchy, wholemeal crust for the pasty, tasteless dough made with refined white flour, and you've already added protein, fibre and vitamins. There are a variety of ways you can make this crust, both with and without yeast. It is a good idea, if the topping is going to be rather liquid, to bake the base in the oven for ten minutes first, so that it does not absorb too much liquid. If, however, you are not too fussed about such details, forget it – there are people who prefer their pizzas this way! You can also bake the dough until completely cooked, then add the topping and heat through briefly in the oven or under the grill – ideal if the topping ingredients do not need cooking (or if you simply prefer to get the maximum goodness from them, and eat them virtually raw). Always grease your baking sheet lightly before putting the dough onto it; you can also brush a light film of oil over the pizza base before adding the topping, and a little more oil over the actual topping ingredients (delicate vegetables such as mushrooms have a tendency to dry out if not protected this way).

How you shape your pizza is also up to you. Traditionally, pizzas are round and you can make one per person, or a large version to be served in slices. You can also make your dough oblong in shape and cook it in a Swiss roll tin, then cut into slices.

For even quicker pizzas, use wholemeal bread, Greek pitta bread, crispbreads or crackers as your base – add tomatoes, cheese, herbs, etc. and simply pop under the grill for a few minutes.

Deep-dish pizzas are not made on a baking sheet, but in a flan dish. The proportion of ingredients is therefore changed so that you have less dough and more filling, and they are served in wedges (although again, you could make very small individual ones and serve one to each person).

The traditional southern Italian pizza contained tomatoes and cheese, usually mozarella and/or Parmesan. In other
parts of Italy the ingredients changed according to what was
available locally, but these basics still tended to be used even if
in lesser amounts. They also occur in many of the recipes in this
book, but you can vary them as you (and your family) like.
Quantities, too, can be adapted to fit in with what you have
available – unlike many recipes, pizzas really cannot go wrong. If
you use wholesome fresh ingredients, and don't overcook them,
the results are bound to be tasty.

When you have learned to be adventurous with your pizza
making, try experimenting with ideas of your own. Most
vegetables, steamed or *sautéed*, make a moist contrast to the
crisp dough. Other cheeses will change the character completely
– try Danish blue, Gruyère, ricotta. Or forget about cheese
altogether and sprinkle your pizza with cooked beans, lightly
fried breadcrumbs, poached or scrambled eggs or bean sprouts.
Many left-overs can be mashed, flavoured with herbs, and put
under the grill for a few minutes to make an unusual topping for
pizza. Soya meat in a thick sauce, or mixed with other ingredients,
adds lots of protein as well as flavour. Tofu bean curd can be
chopped, lightly fried, mixed with vegetables and sesame seeds,
and spread over the dough. Nuts, seeds, herbs, spices – each will
add something different and unique. The variations are restricted
only by the obvious stipulation that you do not top your pizza
with anything too liquid (it will drain away) or too chunky (it will
slide off!). And watch the cooking temperature – the dough
needs a hot oven to cook properly, so if this is likely to ruin the
topping, add it just before the dough is cooked, or cook it
separately and pile on just before serving.

Cold pizzas can be quite as appetizing as hot ones. Use any
left-overs as a party nibble, T.V. snack or instead of biscuits with
coffee. A carefully wrapped slice will help brighten a lunch box
(and break the sandwich syndrome!). Take cold pizza on a picnic
or a ramble; serve it to unexpected guests on a salad or with

soup. You can even heat it up again – add a little extra grated cheese or tomato *purée* and put it under the grill. And you can, of course, freeze any extra pizzas so that they are ready and waiting for the next time you fancy one.

If you haven't tried sweet pizzas, now is your chance. Like a crisp, biscuit-type flan base, the dough lends itself well to such combinations as fruit, jams and honey, nuts, etc., and it really isn't necessary to sweeten it (though you can, of course, if you prefer). Stick to the crisper kind of dough as pizzas served this way should be light and tasty rather than heavy and filling. Make them into small individual circles, or cook them in a Swiss roll tin and slice them before dishing up. The recipes here can be eaten hot or cold, as they are or with yogurt, cream or nut cream. Quantities are half of those suggested for savoury pizzas on the assumption that they will be a delicious 'extra' rather than the main part of the meal; you can always, of course, double the quantities (any left-overs, as with savouries, will be more than edible when cold).

All recipes are for 4 people.

BASIC DOUGH RECIPES

COOKED-IN-THE-PAN PIZZA

6 oz (175g) plain wholemeal flour
1 good teaspoonful baking powder
Water to mix
Sea salt to taste
Vegetable oil for cooking

1. Mix together the flour, baking powder and salt in a bowl.

2. Add water gradually, kneading to make a dough.

3. Continue kneading until dough is smooth and soft, then divide into two, and roll out into thin rounds.

4. Pour a little oil into a heavy pan and heat until hot but not smoking, then turn down heat and cook pizza slowly for two minutes.

5. Turn the pizza, add topping, and continue cooking for a few minutes more, by which time the underside should be brown, and the topping hot right through.

Note: Makes 2 medium-sized or 3 small pizzas.

PIZZA SICILIAN
(fat and filling)

¼ pt (150 ml) warm water
8 oz (225g) plain wholemeal flour
½ tablespoonful dried yeast
1 tablespoonful vegetable oil
½ teaspoonful demerara raw cane sugar

1. Pour the water into a bowl and sprinkle on the yeast. Stir in the sugar, and set aside for 5 to 10 minutes, or until mixture is frothy.

2. Add the oil, then stir the liquid into the sifted flour.

3. Turn onto a floured board and use hands to knead the dough thoroughly until pliable and smooth.

4. Put dough in a greased bowl, cover with a damp cloth, and leave in a warm, draught-free spot until well risen. (Alternatively, you could lightly oil the surface of the dough and put it in a polythene bag, securing the end firmly.)

5. Knead briefly again, then divide dough into four and shape into circles: place on lightly greased baking sheets and return to a warm spot for 15-30 minutes more.

6. Bake blind at 400°F/205°C (Gas Mark 6) for 5 minutes or so to firm up the crust before adding the topping –this helps prevent it becoming soggy.

7. Add topping of your choice and cook 10-15 minutes more.

8. If the topping does not need to be cooked, but just heated through, you can bake the pizza dough for approximately 20 minutes, then add the topping ingredients immediately and put the pizza under the grill for a few minutes more.

Note: Makes 2 medium-sized or 4 small pizzas.

PIZZA NEAPOLITAN
(thin and crisp)

¼ pt (150 ml) warm water
8 oz (225 g) plain wholemeal flour
½ teaspoonful dried yeast
1 tablespoonful vegetable oil

1. Sprinkle the yeast onto the warm water, stir, and set aside until the mixture bubbles.

2. Stir in the oil, then gradually add the liquid to the sifted flour.

3. When this becomes difficult, turn the dough onto a floured board and knead for 5-10 minutes to make a soft, elastic dough.

4. Divide mixture into four, and roll out immediately to make four thin circles.

5. Place on lightly greased baking sheets and pre-bake for 5 minutes at 400°F/205°C (Gas Mark 6).

6. Arrange the topping on the crisp pizza bases and cook for 10-15 minutes more.

7. If the topping does not need to be cooked, but just heated through, you can bake the pizza dough for approximately 20 minutes, then add the topping ingredients and put the pizza under the grill for a few minutes more.

Note: Makes 2 medium-sized or 4 small pizzas.

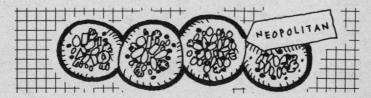

SCONE DOUGH PIZZA

8 oz (225g) self-raising wholemeal flour
2 oz (50g) polyunsaturated margarine
Approx. ¼ pt (150ml) milk
Pinch of sea salt

1. Sieve together the flour and salt.

2. Rub the margarine into the dry ingredients to make a crumb-like mixture.

3. Pour in enough milk to bind the mixture into a soft, manageable dough.

4. Turn onto a floured board and knead lightly.

5. Divide the dough into two and shape into thin rounds.

6. Arrange topping attractively, and bake pizzas at 400°F/205°C (Gas Mark 6) for 20-30 minutes, or until cooked.

Note: Makes 2 medium-sized or 4 small pizzas.

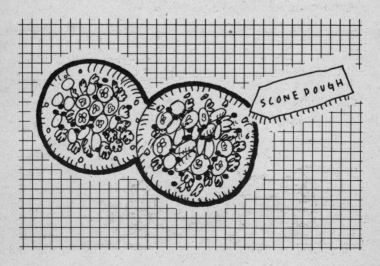

PROTEIN-RICH PIZZA DOUGH

6 oz (175g) plain wholemeal flour
2 oz (50g) soya flour
1 tablespoonful dried yeast
¼ pt (150ml) warm water
1 tablespoonful vegetable oil
½ teaspoonful honey
Pinch of sea salt

1. Pour the water into a bowl, add the yeast and honey, and stir until both have dissolved.

2. Add the oil.

3. Sift together the flours and salt, and gradually add to the liquid, mixing well.

4. Turn dough onto a floured board and knead until supple.

5. Put in a greased bowl, cover, and leave in a warm place for 1 to 2 hours, or until doubled in size.

6. Knead again, then divide into four and shape into circles.

7. Roll out to about ⅛ in. thick and place on baking sheets.

8. Add topping and bake at 425°F/220°C (Gas Mark 7) for 15-20 minutes.

Note: Makes 2 medium-sized or 4 small pizzas.

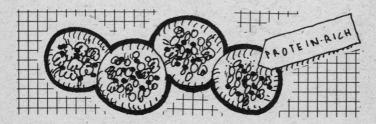

TOPPING IDEAS

PIZZA WITH ADUKI BEANS

Dough for 2 large or 4 small pizzas
8 oz (225 g) aduki beans
1 teaspoonful thyme
1 teaspoonful ground coriander
Pinch of nutmeg
Vegetable oil or polyunsaturated margarine – optional
2 large tomatoes
12 green olives
Seasoning to taste

1. Soak beans overnight, then cook in plenty of water until soft.

2. Make up the pizza bases according to instructions.

3. Drain the beans and mash, or put into a blender, to make a smooth thick *purée*.

4. Stir in the spices and seasoning and, if the mixture seems too dry, just a little oil or margarine.

5. Smooth onto prepared pizza bases and top with slices of tomato and halved, stoned olives.

6. Bake at 400°F/205°C (Gas Mark 6) for approximately 20 minutes, or until base is crisp.

CREAMY MUSHROOM PIZZA

Dough for 2 large or 4 small pizzas
1 large onion
½ clove garlic
12 oz (350 g) firm mushrooms
1 tablespoonful vegetable oil
1 oz (25 g) plain wholemeal flour
½ pt (275 ml) creamy milk, milk with 1 tablespoonful
    skimmed milk powder added, or soya milk
1-2 teaspoonsful dill
Chives to garnish
Seasoning to taste

1. Prepare the pizza bases; bake blind for 15 minutes.

2. Clean and slice the mushrooms; steam briefly, then drain well.

3. Chop the onion finely, then *sauté* for a minute or two with the crushed garlic in the vegetable oil.

4. Add the flour and cook until it begins to colour.

5. Remove from heat; pour in the milk; return to cooker and bring to boil, stirring continually.

6. Add mushrooms, herbs and seasoning; simmer until sauce thickens.

7. Pour onto pizza bases and spread evenly; (if sauce is too thick, add more liquid; if too runny, thicken with a little fine oatmeal).

8. Sprinkle with chopped chives and cook until heated through.

PIZZA 'SCAPRICCIATELLO'

Dough for 2 large or 4 small pizzas
8 oz (225g) ripe tomatoes
4 oz (100g) mozzarella cheese
2 oz (50g) ham-flavoured soya 'meat chunks'
1 medium red pepper
4 oz (100g) mushrooms
1 tablespoonful vegetable oil
20 green olives
1 small tin artichokes or fresh equivalent
4 oz (100g) grated Parmesan cheese
1-2 teaspoonsful oregano
Seasoning to taste

1. Prepare pizza bases, bake blind for 10 minutes, and set aside.

2. Clean, slice and lightly fry the mushrooms. Drain on a paper towel.

3. Hydrate the soya meat, according to pack instructions.

4. Distribute the soya meat, sliced artichokes and mushrooms across the pizza bases.

5. Peel and mash the tomatoes; spread them over the other ingredients and sprinkle with oregano. Season well.

6. Slice the mozzarella thinly and lay on top of pizzas, then arrange olives and strips of pepper over cheese. Sprinkle with Parmesan.

7. Bake for 10 minutes more until mozzarella melts, and dough is completely cooked.

POTATO PIZZA

Dough for 2 large or 4 small pizzas
8 small potatoes, preferably new
1lb (450g) ripe tomatoes
2 large onions
1 tablespoonful vegetable oil
1 tablespoonful basil or oregano
1 clove crushed garlic
Grated Parmesan cheese
10 olives
Parsley to garnish
Seasoning to taste

1. Make up the pizza bases and set aside.

2. Steam the potatoes until just tender, cool slightly, then slice as thin as possible and arrange attractively on pizza dough.

3. Heat the vegetable oil and lightly *sauté* the sliced onion and garlic for 3 minutes.

4. Wash and chop the tomatoes and add to the onion with herbs and seasoning; cook until mixture is thick, and most of the liquid has dried up.

5. Pour sauce over potatoes, spreading it evenly. Sprinkle with cheese, decorate with halved, stoned olives and bake at 400°F/205°C (Gas Mark 6) for 20-25 minutes.

6. Garnish with fresh, chopped parsley.

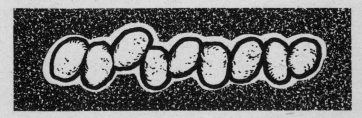

FENNEL PIZZA

Dough for 2 large or 4 small pizzas
1½lb (675g) fennel bulbs of similar size
1 medium onion
½ clove garlic
4oz (100g) polyunsaturated margarine
2 tablespoonsful vegetable oil
1-2 teaspoonsful basil
4oz grated Parmesan cheese
3 large ripe tomatoes
Parsley to garnish
Seasoning to taste

1. Prepare the pizza dough and bake blind for 10 minutes.

2. Remove the outer leaves and stems from the fennel bulbs, wash, cut into quarters, and dry well.

3. In a saucepan melt 2oz (50g) margarine with the oil, then add the fennel and cook gently for a few minutes.

4. Add a spoonful or two of water, cover pan, and simmer for 20 minutes, or until tender.

5. In another pan, heat 2oz (50g) margarine, add the sliced onion and crushed garlic, and cook briefly.

6. Chop or mash the peeled tomatoes and add to the onion, with the basil and seasoning. Cook until a sauce-like mixture forms.

7. Arrange the drained fennel on the pizza bases, and spread with the tomato sauce; top with grated Parmesan and heat for 10 minutes more.

8. Serve garnished with chopped parsley.

CABBAGE AND NUT PIZZA

Dough for 2 large or 4 small pizzas
½ medium white cabbage
4 oz (100g) cream or curd cheese
2 oz (50g) almonds
1 teaspoonful marjoram
1 teaspoonful oregano
Seasoning to taste

1. Prepare pizza bases, bake blind for 15 minutes, and set aside.

2. Shred the cabbage very fine and steam until just tender, then drain.

3. Stir the cheese into the cabbage until it melts, then add seasoning and herbs.

4. Spoon mixture onto pizzas and spread evenly.

5. Chop nuts coarsely and scatter over top.

6. Heat through for 5-10 minutes.

LEEK AND TAHINI PIZZA

Dough for 2 large or 4 small pizzas
1 lb (450 g) leeks
1 tablespoonful vegetable oil
1 oz (25 g) plain wholemeal flour
Barely ⅓ pt (200 ml) cold water
3-4 tablespoonsful tahini sesame paste
Soy sauce to taste
2 oz (50 g) sesame seeds, raw or roasted

1. Prepare pizza bases and bake blind for 15 minutes.

2. Clean and chop the leeks, steam until just tender, drain well.

3. Make a *béchamel* sauce by heating the oil and stirring in the flour until browned, then adding water and bringing to boil.

4. When sauce thickens, remove from heat and add soy sauce and tahini to taste.

5. Stir in the leeks and divide the mixture between the pizzas, spreading it evenly.

6. Sprinkle with sesame seeds.

7. Heat through for the minimum time – in fact, if base is cooked and hot, you can just add the leek topping and serve immediately.

COTTAGE CHEESE PIZZA

Dough for 2 large or 4 small pizzas
1 large onion
1 large red pepper
1 tablespoonful vegetable oil
12 oz (350g) cottage cheese
3 tablespoonsful plain yogurt
2 tablespoonsful capers
20 black olives
1 teaspoonful oregano
1 teaspoonful basil
Seasoning to taste

1. Prepare pizza dough and bake blind for 5 minutes.

2. Heat the oil and gently fry the sliced onion and pepper, then drain and leave to cool.

3. Beat together the cottage cheese and yogurt until mixture is light and smooth; season well.

4. Mix the onion and pepper slices into the cheese, and spread the mixture evenly across the pizza bases.

5. Sprinkle with herbs; decorate with capers and halved, stoned olives.

6. Bake for about 20 minutes.

EGG PIZZA

Dough for 2 large or 4 small pizzas
6 oz (175 g) Cheddar cheese
6 hard-boiled eggs
4 oz (100g) mushrooms
1 medium onion
4 tablespoonsful tomato *purée*
1 teaspoonful mixed herbs
Pinch of paprika
Seasoning to taste

1. Make up the dough and bake blind for 15 minutes. Cool slightly.

2. Chop onion as finely as possible and mix into the tomato *purée* with the herbs and seasoning.

3. Spread tomato mixture over pizzas.

4. Slice eggs and mushrooms, and arrange decoratively on top of tomato, then sprinkle generously with grated Cheddar cheese.

5. Add pinch of paprika and heat pizzas through quickly until cheese has melted and dough is cooked.

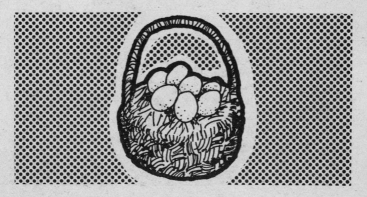

OLIVE PIZZA

Dough for 2 large or 4 small pizzas
6 oz (175 g) green olives
2-3 oz (50-75 g) wholemeal breadcrumbs
3 teaspoonsful lemon juice
1 large red pepper
Seasoning to taste

1. Prepare the dough and bake blind for 15-20 minutes. Keep warm.

2. Meanwhile, remove the stones from the olives and then mince or mash the flesh.

3. Add the breadcrumbs, lemon juice and a generous amount of seasoning, and pound all the ingredients together, preferably in a mortar, so that all are thoroughly mixed.

4. Spread olive paste onto pizza bases, decorate with narrow strips of pepper, and grill for a few minutes until heated through.

ASPARAGUS PIZZA

Dough for 2 large or 4 small pizzas
Approx. 20 cooked asparagus tips
2 medium onions
8 oz (225 g) ripe tomatoes
1 oz (25 g) polyunsaturated margarine
1 tablespoonful vegetable oil
8 oz (225 g) Emmenthal cheese
1-2 teaspoonsful oregano
2 oz (50 g) Parmesan cheese
Parsley to garnish
Seasoning to taste

1. Prepare the pizza dough and bake blind for 5 minutes.

2. Heat the oil and margarine together, add the sliced onion
    and cook for a few minutes, then add the skinned, mashed
    tomatoes.

3. Cook tomato sauce over moderate heat without a cover so
    that most of the liquid evaporates, then combine with the
    drained asparagus tips and heat through for a few minutes
    more.

4. Spoon mixture onto the pizza bases, sprinkle with oregano
    and season well.

5. Top with Emmenthal cheese cut into thin slices, a sprinkling
    of Parmesan cheese and chopped parsley.

6. Bake at 400°F/205°C (Gas Mark 6) for 15-20 minutes.

CHINESE PIZZA

Dough for 2 large or 4 small pizzas
4 oz (100 g) tofu bean curd
4 tablespoonsful tomato *purée*
2 oz (50 g) polyunsaturated margarine
1 small head of celery
4 oz (100 g) cooked peas
1 red pepper
4 oz (100 g) bean sprouts
1 oz (25 g) wholemeal breadcrumbs
Soy sauce
Seasoning to taste

1.   Prepare pizza dough and set aside.

2.   Melt margarine in a frying pan and cook finely sliced celery and pepper for 5 minutes; add cubed tofu and continue cooking, stirring frequently, until tofu begins to brown.

3.   Stir in peas and sprouts, season, sprinkle with soy sauce, and cook a minute or two more.

4.   Sprinkle a little soy sauce into the tomato *purée*, then spread over the pizza bases.

5.   Spoon the vegetable and tofu mixture over the pizzas and top with breadcrumbs – you may like to dot some small pieces of margarine on top of the crumbs.

6.   Bake at 375°F/190°C (Gas Mark 5) for 20 minutes or until dough is cooked.

PIZZA MARGHERITA

Dough for 2 large or 4 small pizzas
6 medium tomatoes
8 oz (225 g) bel paese cheese
1-2 teaspoonsful oregano
Approx. 1 tablespoonful vegetable oil
Seasoning to taste

1. Prepare dough and shape into circles.

2. Slice the tomatoes and place them on the pizza bases.

3. Cover with the thinly sliced cheese, then add herbs and seasoning.

4. Sprinkle a little oil over the top before baking at 400°F/205°C (Gas Mark 6) for about 20 minutes, or until dough is cooked through, and cheese has melted.

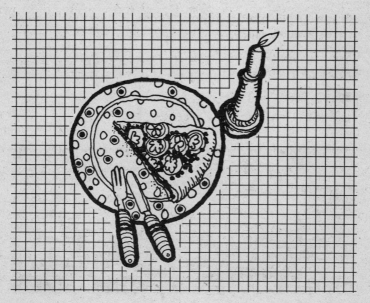

HOT PEPPER PIZZA

Dough for 2 large or 4 small pizzas
2 medium onions
2 medium green peppers
4 medium tomatoes
4 tablespoonsful sweet corn
1 clove garlic, crushed
1-2 tablespoonsful lemon juice
½ teaspoonful chilli powder or to taste
Pinch of raw cane sugar
Seasoning to taste
4 oz (100g) mozzarella cheese

1. Prepare dough for bases and bake blind for 5 minutes.

2. Skin and chop the tomatoes and onions, and put into a small pan with garlic, lemon juice, chilli powder and sugar.

3. Simmer uncovered for about 20 minutes, or until vegetables make a thick sauce.

4. Spread slightly cooled tomato sauce over pizza bases, and top with finely sliced peppers and sweet corn.

5. Season, then add sliced cheese.

6. Bake at 400°F/205°C (Gas Mark 6) for a further 20 minutes.

BROCCOLI PIZZA WITH EGG

Dough for 2 large or 4 small pizzas
10 oz (275 g) fresh or frozen broccoli
3 oz (75 g) polyunsaturated margarine
1 oz (25 g) plain wholemeal flour
½ pt (275 ml) milk
3 hard-boiled eggs
2 oz (50 g) wholemeal breadcrumbs
Parsley
Seasoning to taste

1. Make up pizza bases and cook for 5-10 minutes.

2. Clean, break up and cook broccoli in a steamer, or the minimum of water, until tender; then drain.

3. Melt 1 oz (25 g) of the margarine in a small pan and stir in the flour; cook for a few minutes.

4. Remove pan from the heat and add milk, then bring to boil, stirring continually, to make a thick sauce. Season to taste.

5. Heat the remaining 2 oz (50 g) of margarine in another pan and toss crumbs in the hot fat until crisp.

6. Mix parsley and finely chopped eggs with the crumbs.

7. Spread the broccoli pieces across the pizza bases; pour on the sauce; sprinkle with the egg and breadcrumb mixture.

8. Bake at 400°F/205°C (Gas Mark 6) for about 10 minutes, or until cooked.

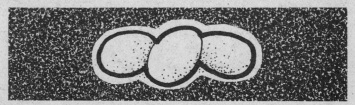

SPINACH PAPRIKA PIZZA

Dough for 2 large or 4 small pizzas
1 lb (450g) fresh or frozen spinach
1 oz (25g) polyunsaturated margarine
1 tablespoonful vegetable oil
½ clove garlic, crushed
1-2 tablespoonsful fresh paprika
Seasoning to taste
4 oz (100g) grated Parmesan cheese
2 oz (50g) wheat germ

1. Make up pizza dough, shape into circles, and bake blind for 20 minutes.

2. Combine the margarine and oil in a saucepan, add the crushed garlic, paprika and seasoning, and cook gently for 5 minutes.

3. Meanwhile, steam the washed, shredded spinach until just tender, then drain well.

4. Put the spinach in with the paprika sauce and heat through, stirring frequently.

5. Pile spinach onto cooked pizza bases, smooth top; sprinkle with cheese and wheat germ mixed together. Either return to the oven, or grill pizzas for a few minutes longer.

PIZZA WITH 'SAUSAGE'

Dough for 2 large or 4 small pizzas
1 tin soya meat 'sausages'
4 oz (100g) mushrooms
4 large tomatoes
2 large onions
1 tablespoonful vegetable oil
1 teaspoonful oregano
3 oz (75g) Cheddar cheese
Seasoning to taste

1. Prepare pizza dough and make into circles.

2. Lightly fry the sliced onions and mushrooms in the oil, then drain on a paper towel.

3. Cut the tomatoes into rings and arrange on the pizza bases, then add the onion and mushroom mixture, distributing it evenly.

4. Chop the drained sausages into thin slices, and place these on top of the pizzas, season well, and sprinkle with oregano.

5. Finally, top with some grated cheese, and bake pizzas at 400°F/205°C (Gas Mark 6) for 20 minutes, or until dough is cooked through.

AUBERGINE PIZZA
(Greek Style)

Dough for 2 large or 4 small pizzas
1 large aubergine
2 tablespoonsful vegetable oil
2 oz (50g) polyunsaturated margarine
1-2 cloves garlic, crushed
1 large onion
6 large ripe tomatoes
2 tablespoonsful lemon juice
Good pinch of nutmeg
Parsley
4 tablespoonsful cooked chick peas
Seasoning to taste

1. Prepare the pizza bases and bake blind for 20 minutes, or until completely cooked.

2. Meanwhile, peel the aubergine and cut the flesh into small cubes.

3. Heat together the oil and margarine, and lightly *sauté* the aubergine, stirring often, remove from pan.

4. In the same pan, cook the sliced onion with the garlic until the onion begins to look transparent.

5. Peel and chop the tomatoes and add to the onion with the aubergine, lemon juice, nutmeg, chopped parsley and seasoning.

6. After bringing the mixture to a boil, reduce the heat and let it simmer, uncovered, for 10-15 minutes, or until most of the liquid has evaporated.

7. Spoon mixture onto hot pizza bases; sprinkle with coarsely chopped chick peas. Serve immediately.

CHEESE AND ONION PIZZA

Dough for 2 large or 4 small pizzas
4 medium onions
1 oz (25 g) polyunsaturated margarine
1 oz (25 g) plain wholemeal flour
2 heaped tablespoonsful skimmed milk powder
4 oz (100 g) Edam cheese
2 oz (50 g) wholemeal breadcrumbs
Approx. 12 green olives
Seasoning to taste

1. Prepare dough for pizza bases and bake blind for 5 minutes.

2. Peel the onions, cut into thick slices, and steam briefly until just tender.

3. Melt the margarine in a pan; add the flour and *sauté* for a few minutes.

4. Drain the onion water into a measuring jug; make up to $1/3$ pint with water if necessary; stir in the powdered milk until dissolved.

5. Add to margarine and flour mixture, bring to boil, then simmer to make a thick sauce. Season to taste.

6. Off the heat, add most of the grated cheese to the sauce, then the onions, and mix well.

7. Spread mixture evenly over the pizza bases.

8. Top with halved, stoned olives, breadcrumbs, and a sprinkling of grated cheese.

9. Bake at 400°F/205°C (Gas Mark 6) for about 20 minutes more.

GORGONZOLA WALNUT PIZZA

Dough for 2 large or 4 small pizzas
4 oz (100g) Gorgonzola cheese
4 oz (100g) polyunsaturated margarine
Good pinch of ground cumin
2 oz (50g) walnut pieces

1. Prepare the pizza dough, then bake blind for 20 minutes.

2. To make Gorgonzola topping, grate the cheese, then mash it together with the margarine and cumin, making sure it is well combined.

3. Spread over top of cooked pizza, sprinkle with chopped walnuts, and grill for a few minutes.

ARTICHOKE PIZZA

Dough for 2 large or 4 small pizzas
2 medium cooked artichokes
2 oz (50g) sesame seeds
1 tablespoonful vegetable oil
½-1 clove garlic, crushed
4 large ripe tomatoes
4 oz (100g) bel paese or mozzarella cheese
1 tablespoonful fresh basil
Seasoning to taste

1. Make up pizza dough; shape into circles; bake blind for 5 minutes.

2. Heat the oil in a small pan, add the garlic and cook briefly.

3. Peel and mash the tomatoes, then put them into the pan with the oil mixture, adding seasoning to taste.

4. Cook for 10 minutes, or until the sauce thickens, then let it cool slightly.

5. Spread tomato sauce over pizza dough; arrange thinly sliced artichokes over the sauce, and sprinkle with seeds.

6. Slice the cheese and distribute decoratively across the top of pizzas.

7. Garnish with chopped basil and bake at 400°F/205°C (Gas Mark 6) for 20 minutes, or until cooked.

PIZZA WITH PEANUT BUTTER TOPPING

Dough for 2 large or 4 small pizzas
4 oz (100g) chunky peanut butter
2 oz (50g) wholemeal breadcrumbs
2 medium carrots
2 medium sticks celery
1 medium onion
1 oz (25g) polyunsaturated margarine
1-2 teaspoonsful marjoram
Seasoning to taste
1 oz (25g) sunflower seeds

1. Prepare the dough, divide and shape as required, and cook the bases blind for 10 minutes.

2. Peel the carrots and onion; slice them and the celery as finely as possible.

3. *Sauté* vegetables in the melted margarine for 5 minutes, or until just tender.

4. In a bowl, and using a wooden spoon, mix together the peanut butter and breadcrumbs to make a paste.

5. Stir in the vegetables, herbs and seasoning; if too dry, add a little water or milk to moisten mixture.

6. Spread over the prepared bases; top with a sprinkling of seeds; return pizzas to the oven for 10 minutes more.

PIZZA FOUR SEASONS

Dough for 2 large or 4 small pizzas
4oz (100g) bel paese cheese
4oz (100g) mushrooms
1 small tin nutmeat
4 large tomatoes
1 tablespoonful vegetable oil
½ clove garlic, crushed
Black olives to garnish
1-2 teaspoonsful oregano
Seasoning to taste

1. Prepare the dough and arrange on a baking sheet.

2. Mentally divide each pizza into four quarters (or mark them
    with strips of pepper). Brush the dough with oil and sprinkle
    with garlic.

3. Slice the mushrooms, arrange some on one quarter of each
    pizza; brush with a little more oil.

4. Do the same with slices of the nutmeat; grate or thinly slice
    the cheese and cover the third quarter of each pizza; spread
    the coarsely chopped tomatoes over the remaining dough
    and sprinkle with oregano; decorate with the olives.

5. Bake at 400°F/200°C (Gas Mark 6) for 20-30 minutes, or
    until cooked.

Note: There are as many variations of this classic pizza as there
are ingredients. For variety try using cooked (or tinned) arti-
choke hearts, fried peppers and onions, sweet corn; or make
your pizza with four different varieties of cheese.

SCRAMBLED EGG PIZZA WITH SWEET CORN

Dough for 2 large or 4 small pizzas
4 eggs
1 oz (25 g) polyunsaturated margarine
6 oz (175 g) cooked and drained sweet corn
Pinch of cayenne pepper
Seasoning to taste
Parsley to garnish

1. Make up the dough; shape into pizzas; bake blind at 400°F/200°C (Gas Mark 6) for 20 minutes or until crisp.

2. In a bowl, beat together the eggs, sweet corn and seasoning.

3. Just before the pizza bases are ready, melt the margarine in a pan, pour in the egg and sweet corn mixture, and cook gently, stirring continually, until the mixture thickens.

4. Remove pizza bases from the oven immediately and spread with the mixture; garnish with plenty of fresh parsley and possibly an extra pinch of paprika. Serve hot.

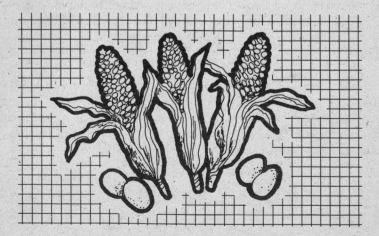

SLOPPY JOE PIZZA

Dough for 2 large or 4 small pizzas
5 oz (150g) soya 'minced meat', hydrated
1 medium green pepper
1 large onion
1 oz (25g) polyunsaturated margarine
1 tablespoonful vegetable oil
1-2 tablespoonsful tomato *purée*
Good pinch of chilli powder or to taste
Seasoning to taste

1. Prepare pizza bases and bake at 400°F/200°C (Gas Mark 6) for 15 minutes.

2. At the same time, melt the margarine in a pan with the oil; gently *sauté* the sliced pepper and onion for 5 minutes, or until just softening.

3. Add the drained 'minced meat' with the tomato *purée* and seasoning; mix well; simmer for 10 minutes.

4. Spoon mixture over pizza bases (if it is too liquid you can either drain off some of the excess juices, or thicken it with some breadcrumbs, rolled oats, or flour).

5. Return pizzas to the oven for approximately 10 minutes more.

Note: This – as the name implies – is not the kind of pizza you can eat in your hand!

COURGETTE PIZZA

Dough for 2 large or 4 small pizzas
4 large courgettes
4 oz (100g) wholemeal breadcrumbs
4 oz (100g) Cheddar cheese
1-2 teaspoonsful sage
2 oz (50g) lightly roasted peanuts
Seasoning to taste
2 oz (50g) melted polyunsaturated margarine

1. Prepare the dough; shape into individual pizzas; set aside.

2. Chop the washed courgettes as finely as possible; in a bowl combine them thoroughly with the breadcrumbs, grated cheese, sage, seasoning, and half of the melted margarine.

3. Spread the mixture over the pizza dough; sprinkle with the peanuts (whole or coarsely chopped); trickle the remaining fat over the top.

4. Bake at 400°F/200°C (Gas Mark 6) for 20-30 minutes, or until the dough is cooked, and the top golden and bubbly.

MUSHROOM AND YOGURT PIZZA

Dough for 2 large or 4 small pizzas
12 oz (350g) mushrooms
2 small cartons plain yogurt
1-2 tablespoonsful vegetable oil
1 medium onion – optional
6 oz (175g) Cheddar cheese
Seasoning to taste
Chives to garnish

1. Make up the dough and shape pizzas; bake blind at 400°F/200°C (Gas Mark 6) for 20-30 minutes or until cooked.

2. Wash, dry and slice the mushrooms; *sauté* briefly in the oil, then drain well; *sauté* sliced onion if using it; mix with mushrooms.

3. Distribute mushrooms over pizzas and season to taste; spoon on the yogurt; add grated cheese.

4. Grill pizzas lightly until top is browned; decorate with chives before serving.

Note: This is a creamy, smooth-tasting pizza. If you like your food with more flavour, add the onion.

ALMOND PIZZA

2 oz (50g) ground almonds
Barely ¹/₃ pt (200ml) creamy milk
6 oz (175g) grated Cheddar cheese
2 oz (50g) wholemeal breadcrumbs
2 large tomatoes
1 tablespoonful vegetable oil
Seasoning to taste

1. Make up the dough; bake blind for 10 minutes at 400°F/200°C (Gas Mark 6).

2. Blend together the ground almonds, creamy milk, grated cheese and seasoning to make a thick sauce.

3. Heat the oil and fry the breadcrumbs with the chopped tomatoes until the crumbs are crisp.

4. Spread the almond and cheese mixture evenly over the pizza dough; sprinkle with the crumbs and tomatoes; return to the oven for 10-20 minutes until cooked.

Note: Other nuts, especially hazels and walnuts, go well with this recipe; mushrooms can replace the tomatoes in the topping.

PARSNIP AND ONION PIZZA

Dough for 2 large or 4 small pizzas
4 medium parsnips, sliced and steamed
2 medium onions
2 oz (50g) polyunsaturated margarine
½ clove garlic, crushed
2 oz (50g) walnut pieces
Seasoning to taste

1. Make up the basic dough; shape into pizzas; bake at 400°F/200°C (Gas Mark 6) for 15-20 minutes.

2. Melt the margarine and add the garlic, onions, and chopped walnut pieces; cook for 5-10 minutes until the onions are tender.

3. Drain the parsnip slices and add to the pan; continue to cook over a low heat, turning frequently.

4. When parsnips are lightly browned season to taste; then spoon mixture evenly over the pizza dough.

5. Return to oven for 5-10 minutes more.

OMELETTE 'PIZZA'

6 eggs
4 tablespoonsful plain yogurt
1 tablespoonful vegetable oil
1 large onion
1 large green pepper
3 large tomatoes
4 oz (100g) Parmesan cheese
Black olives to garnish
2 teaspoonsful oregano
Seasoning to taste

1. Whisk together the eggs, yogurt and seasoning; heat half the oil in a large frying pan; pour in the egg mixture and cook gently until lightly set underneath.

2. Turn on the grill and continue cooking the omelette this way so that the top sets (be careful not to overcook it).

3. At the same time, *sauté* the sliced onion and pepper in the rest of the oil until just tender.

4. Using the omelette as a pizza base, arrange the vegetables, sliced tomatoes and olives across the top. Season, add herbs and sprinkle with grated cheese.

5. Return omelette pizza to the grill for just a few minutes more. Serve in slices.

Note: This is obviously not a real pizza – just an unusual way to serve the traditional pizza ingredients. You can, if you prefer, cook your pizza dough in the usual way, and the omelette as described above. Spread some tomato *purée* or sauce over the cooked dough, chop the omelette into fine strips and arrange them on top, sprinkle with cheese and grill briefly.

SPLIT PEA PIZZA

Dough for 2 large or 4 small pizzas
6 oz (175g) split green peas, soaked overnight
2 oz (50g) cooked brown rice
1 large onion
1 tablespoonful vegetable oil
Soy sauce
2 tablespoonsful soured cream or margarine or tahini
2 large tomatoes

1. Heat the oil in a pan and *sauté* the sliced onion for 5 minutes; stir in the drained split peas with a little fresh water to cover them and a good sprinkling of soy sauce. Cover and simmer until the peas form a soft, thick *purée*.

2. Make up the dough; shape into pizzas; bake at 400°F/200°C (Gas Mark 6) for 15 minutes.

3. Use a wooden spoon to mash the peas, add the rice, then stir in the cream or margarine for a smoother taste; spread mixture over base; top with sliced tomatoes arranged attractively.

4. Return pizza to oven and bake for 5-10 minutes more.

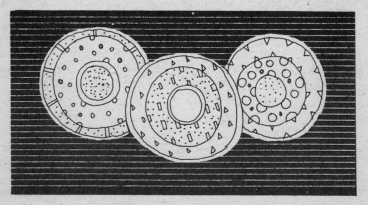

SUNFLOWER SEED PIZZA

Dough for 2 large or 4 small pizzas
1 large green pepper
2 large onions
3 sticks celery
2 tablespoonsful vegetable oil
1 teaspoonful yeast extract, or to taste
1 teaspoonful mixed herbs
3-4 oz (75-100g) sunflower seeds, ground to a meal
Seasoning to taste

1. Prepare dough; divide into pizzas; bake blind for 10 minutes at 400°F/200°C (Gas Mark 6).

2. Heat the oil in a pan and gently *sauté* the sliced pepper, onions and celery until just becoming tender.

3. Dissolve the yeast extract in the minimum of water and add to the pan with seasoning and herbs; cook a little longer, stirring occasionally.

4. Mix in the meal, which should soak up most of the liquid; if the mixture is still very wet you can add more meal, or a spoonful or two of oats.

5. Spread mixture over the pizza dough; bake for 10-20 minutes more, or until the dough is cooked.

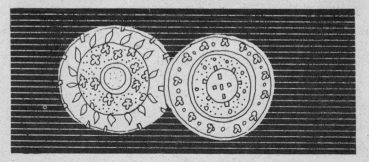

DEEP-DISH PIZZA

For Pastry
6 oz (175 g) plain wholemeal flour
3 oz (75 g) polyunsaturated margarine
Approx. 2 tablespoonsful cold water
Seasoning to taste

For Filling
6 oz (175 g) Cheddar cheese
½ oz (15 g) polyunsaturated margarine
½ oz (15 g) plain wholemeal flour
¼ pt (150 ml) milk
1 teaspoonful marjoram
4 oz (100 g) mushrooms
4 tomatoes
6 green olives
Seasoning to taste

1. Sieve the flour and seasoning together; use fingertips to rub in the margarine; add enough water to make a smooth dough.

2. Roll out the dough and use to line a flan ring or tin; bake blind for 15 minutes at 400°F/200°C (Gas Mark 6).

3. Meanwhile, melt the margarine in a pan, sprinkle in the flour and cook until golden; stir in milk and continue cooking until sauce thickens.

4. Add 4 oz (100 g) of grated cheese to the sauce; season and add herbs.

5. Wash and slice mushrooms, layer over the base of the flan; pour on the slightly cooled sauce.

6. Arrange sliced tomatoes and halved olives on top, sprinkle with cheese.

7. Continue baking for about 10 minutes more or until pastry is cooked and crisp. Serve in wedges.

WELSH RAREBIT PIZZA

Dough for 2 large or 4 small pizzas
2 oz (50g) polyunsaturated margarine
1 oz (25g) plain wholemeal flour
1 lb (450g) Cheddar, Cheshire or Edam cheese
¼ pt (150 ml) milk
2 egg yolks
Pinch of nutmeg and dry mustard
Seasoning to taste

1. Roll out the dough; shape into pizzas; bake blind at
    400°F/200°C (Gas Mark 6) for 20-25 minutes, or until just
    cooked.

2. Melt the margarine and stir in the flour; cook for 5 minutes
    over a low heat.

3. Add the milk, bring to the boil, and continue cooking until
    the sauce begins to thicken; add grated cheese, egg yolks,
    and seasoning, and continue cooking to make a thick,
    smooth sauce.

4. Spread over the cooked pizza dough and put under a hot
    grill for just a few minutes to brown.

Note: Any sauce not used can be kept for a while in the
refrigerator in a screw-top jar. Adapt this basic recipe by using a
little ale instead of some of the milk; by varying the cheeses; by
topping the dough with a few bean sprouts, soya 'bacon'-
flavoured Smokey Snaps, or lightly fried mushrooms, then
pouring on the sauce; or arrange poached eggs or sliced
tomatoes on top of the sauce.

PIZZA WITH RATATOUILLE

Dough for 2 large or 4 small pizzas
1 large green pepper
1 large aubergine
2 large courgettes
2 large onions
2 large tomatoes
1 clove garlic, crushed
2 tablespoonsful vegetable oil
Chopped parsley to garnish
2 oz (50g) flaked almonds or 2 oz (50g) grated Cheddar
  cheese
Seasoning to taste

1. Make up the dough in the usual way; arrange on baking
   sheet; cook for 15 minutes at 400°F/200°C (Gas Mark 6).

2. Meanwhile, make the ratatouille: coarsely chop tomatoes,
   peel the onions, then slice with the rest of the vegetables;
   sauté with the crushed garlic in the oil until tender.

3. Spoon drained ratatouille over pizza dough and sprinkle
   with nuts or cheese; return to the oven for 10 minutes more,
   or until dough is cooked. Serve garnished with plenty of
   parsley.

CINNAMON NUT PIZZA

Dough for 1 large or 2 small pizzas
4 oz (100g) polyunsaturated margarine
1 oz (25g) wholemeal flour
4 oz (100g) demerara raw cane sugar
Approx. 1 tablespoonful cinnamon
2 oz (50g) mixed chopped nuts

1. Prepare the dough; make up into one large or two small pizzas; arrange on baking sheet.

2. In a bowl, rub the flour and 3 oz (75g) of the margarine together, then stir in the spice and sugar.

3. Melt the remaining fat and brush the pizza top with it generously.

4. Mix the nuts into the topping and sprinkle it over the pizza; bake at 400°F/200°C (Gas Mark 6) for 20-30 minutes, or until dough is crisp and cooked through.

APPLE AND GINGER PIZZA

Dough for 1 large or 2 small pizzas
1 lb (450g) cooking apples, peeled and cored
Approx. 2 oz (50g) light muscovado raw cane sugar
½ oz (15g) polyunsaturated margarine
4 oz (100g) wholemeal ginger biscuits

1. Make up dough; shape into circles; bake blind at 400°F/200° (Gas Mark 6) for 10 minutes.

2. Meanwhile make a thick apple *purée* by simmering the finely sliced apples with sugar, the minimum of water and the margarine.

3. When cooked, mash to a pulp with a wooden spoon; drain off excess juice.

4. Spread apple *purée* over partially cooked pizza base; sprinkle with coarsely crushed biscuits; return to oven for 10-20 minutes, or until dough is browned and crisp.

Note: This sweet pizza makes a tasty change from apple pie. Serve it in slices, possibly with cream that has been whipped then flavoured with some finely sliced preserved ginger (the variety preserved in honey is especially good) and a little of the ginger syrup.

PINEAPPLE COTTAGE CHEESE PIZZA

Dough for 1 large or 2 small pizzas
1 8oz (225g) carton cottage cheese with pineapple or plain cottage cheese plus 2oz (50g) cubed or crushed fresh pineapple
2 tablespoonsful plain yogurt
1oz (25g) demerara raw cane sugar – optional

1. Make up the dough and divide into separate portions; shape into circles.

2. Combine cottage cheese, pineapple and yogurt, and spread evenly over dough; sprinkle with sugar if desired.

3. Bake at 400°F/200°C (Gas Mark 6) for 20 minutes, or until cooked.

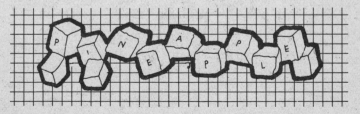

BANANA PIZZA

Dough for 1 large or 2 small pizzas
4-5 large ripe bananas
Good squeeze of lemon juice
2 tablespoonsful pure maple syrup
2 oz (50g) walnut pieces

1. Make up the pizza dough and bake blind for 20-30 minutes (or until cooked) at 400°F/200°C (Gas Mark 6).

2. Shortly before the pizza base is cooked, peel and mash the bananas with the lemon juice; then add maple syrup to taste and combine well.

3. Take pizza from the oven and spread with the banana *purée*; sprinkle with chopped walnuts.

4. Serve immediately, or return pizza to oven for literally a few minutes to heat the topping.

Note: If desired, you can make a thicker, creamier topping by mashing a little whipped cream, yogurt, sour cream or tofu with the bananas and syrup.

MINCEMEAT PIZZA

Dough for 1 large or 2 small pizzas
6 oz (175g) raw sugar mincemeat*
2 dessert pears

1. Prepare dough as usual; shape as desired; arrange on baking sheet.

2. Peel, core and chop the pears into small pieces, then mix well with the mincemeat. (If it seems dry, add a little fruit juice.)

3. Spread the mixture over the pizza and bake at 400°F/200°C (Gas Mark 6) for 20-30 minutes, or until cooked.

To make mincemeat
2 oz (50g) melted polyunsaturated margarine
1 small dessert apple, grated
8 oz (225g) mixed dried fruit
2 oz (50g) mixed dried peel
2 oz (50g) demerara raw cane sugar
2 oz (50g) chopped nuts
Juice and grated rind of ½ a lemon
½ teaspoonful mixed spice
½ teaspoonful nutmeg or cinnamon
2 tablespoonsful orange juice

1. If you need to wash the dried fruit, make sure it is completely dry; then mix all the ingredients together; put into a clean jar and seal.

Note: This quantity makes just over 1 lb (450g) mincemeat. If you wish to make a larger quantity, double the ingredients, preferably replacing the orange juice with brandy, sherry or rum as mincemeat made with alcohol in this way will keep much longer.

CREAMY COCONUT PIZZA

Dough for 1 large or 2 small pizzas
2 oz (50 g) polyunsaturated margarine
2 oz (50 g) light muscovado raw cane sugar
3 oz (75 g) desiccated coconut
3 tablespoonsful double cream or sieved cottage cheese
   or cream cheese

1. Prepare and shape dough into circles or use to line a Swiss roll tin; bake at 400°F/200°C (Gas Mark 6) for 20-30 minutes.

2. In a bowl mix together the margarine, sugar and coconut; add the cream and blend thoroughly.

3. When pizza base is cooked, spread the mixture over it evenly and put under a grill for just a few minutes until the topping is golden and bubbly. Serve immediately as a dessert, or – if baking in a Swiss roll tin – cut into slices, allow to cool, and serve as a cake.

DATE AND NUT PIZZA

Dough for 1 large or 2 small pizzas
8 oz (225 g) dates
2 teaspoonsful lemon juice
2 oz (50 g) chopped roasted hazelnuts
1 oz (25 g) sunflower seeds
1 oz (25 g) desiccated coconut – optional

1. Prepare the dough; shape and set out on baking sheet.

2. Chop the dates into small pieces, put into a pan with the lemon juice and a few spoonsful of water; simmer until they form a paste. (You may need to add more water, and should stir frequently to break up the fruit.)

3. Spread the thick paste evenly over the dough and top with the nuts, seeds and coconut if using it; bake at 400°F/200°C (Gas Mark 6) for 20 minutes or until dough is cooked.

Note: For variety, mix the dates with apple *purée* or use different types of nuts.

PIZZA WITH FRESH FRUIT

Dough for 1 large or 2 small pizzas
12 oz (350g) fresh fruit (e.g. blackberries, cherries, peaches,
   melon, pineapple, white grapes – you need a
   combination)
¼ pt (150ml) fruit juice
1 teaspoonful arrowroot

1. Make up the dough for the base; shape as required; bake
    blind at 400°F/200°C (Gas Mark 6) for 20 minutes, or until
    completely cooked. Set aside to cool.

2. Chop the fruit if necessary to make a fruit salad type of
    mixture.

3. Mix the arrowroot with the fruit juice, put into a saucepan,
    and bring to boil; then simmer until the sauce thickens.

4. When sauce is cool, add fruit and mix well, then arrange
    fruit across pizza dough; pour on any extra fruit glaze. Serve
    in wedges with cream or yogurt.

Note: If you prefer, you can use the pizza base whilst still hot;
warm the fruit by adding it to the sauce, whilst it is cooking.
Simmer for a few minutes and serve with custard. A few drops of
almond essence mixed into the sauce give it a very special
flavour too.

APRICOT CRUNCH PIZZA

Dough for 1 large or 2 small pizzas
8 oz (225 g) dried apricot halves, soaked overnight
4 tablespoonsful raw sugar apricot jam
Approx. 4 tablespoonsful crunchy oat cereal

1. Make pizza dough and bake pizza blind at 400°F/200°C (Gas Mark 6) for 10 minutes.

2. If the apricot halves are tender, use them without cooking; if, however, they are still too chewy, simmer them in a little water for 10 minutes.

3. Gently heat the jam with some of the water in which the apricots were soaked or cooked, to make a thick sauce.

4. Arrange the drained apricot halves decoratively in circles over the dough; pour a little of the apricot sauce over them, spreading it as evenly as possible; sprinkle on the coarsely crumbled cereal.

5. Return pizza to the oven for 10-20 minutes more, until dough is cooked.

PIZZA WITH CHESTNUT PURÉE

Dough for 1 large or 2 small pizzas
12 oz (350g) chestnuts or 1 tin unsweetened chestnut *purée*
2 oz (50g) raw cane sugar, powdered in grinder
¼-½ pt (150-275 ml) whipping cream
A little raw sugar chocolate or freshly ground coffee

1. Cut the end of each chestnut, then boil in water for about 30 minutes; remove outer and inner skins; mash, sieve or blend the flesh to make a *purée*.

2. Bake the prepared pizza dough at 400°F/200°C (Gas Mark 6) for 20 minutes, or until completely cooked; set aside to cool.

3. Whip the cream, then add half of it to the chestnut *purée* with the sugar, and beat thoroughly.

4. Spread the cooled mixture over the pizza base and decorate with the rest of the cream; or serve it separately for everyone to help themselves. Sprinkle the pizza with some grated chocolate or, the Italian way, with freshly ground coffee.

Note: This pizza can also be served hot. Cook the base for just 10 minutes, then add the sweetened chestnut *purée* and return the pizza to the oven for as long as it takes for the base to cook; serve the cream in a jug. If serving it cold, you can adjust the amount of cream to suit your own tastes – anything from a spoonful to a pint!

MAKING PANCAKES

Considering the fact that pancakes date back to the Middle Ages, it perhaps isn't surprising that they are eaten today in just about every country, and in a wide variety of guises. Although in many cases they form part of the staple day-to-day diet, in Britain they have long been thought of as a once-a-year treat, appearing only on Shrove Tuesday as tradition demands – and delighting everyone. More recently, however, a number of restaurants specializing in both sweet and savoury pancakes have sprung up, and have opened up thrifty housewives' eyes to the endless possibilities of these simple, tasty and inexpensive pan-cooked 'cakes'.

One of the best things about them is their versatility. They can be fat and filling, light and lacy; can be served as breakfast, lunch, dinner, T.V. snack – you can even make them into a cake and decorate them with birthday candles! Once you get used to cooking them (and it's really much easier than you may think) you can dish them up to your family regularly – vary the fillings and no one will get bored with pancakes; make them with natural, wholesome ingredients, and you can be sure you're giving everyone the nutrients they need as well as the treat they deserve.

In theory, pancakes are bigger, thicker, and therefore more likely to have savoury fillings, whilst *crêpes* are usually no more than four inches wide, light and crisp, and are ideal for desserts or light snacks. If you eat out, you'll often find there's little difference between the two, and there are certainly no hard and fast rules. Use whatever batter you prefer, make your pancakes fat or thin, huge or saucer-sized and fill them with whatever you have handy. Although most of the batter recipes given here do not contain sugar, you can add sweetener if you wish; you can also add chopped nuts, grated raw sugar chocolate or carob powder, essences such as almond or vanilla, or even substitute orange juice for the milk in the batter mix.

For savoury pancakes, mix in some sesame, caraway or sunflower seeds (whole or ground), a little grated cheese, bean sprouts, herbs, bran or wheatgerm, curry powder or spices. For a crisper texture to your pancake, add a spoonful of vegetable oil.

Ingredients for the batter should obviously be as fresh as possible. Plain flour has a higher gluten content than self-raising (though you *can* use either); use 100% wholemeal and, if you find it too coarse, sift out some of the bran. Milk or cream give a richer batter, soya milk or water a lighter pancake; make it without eggs if your prefer, or add as many as you like within reason (for a really light pancake separate the eggs and fold the stiffly beaten whites in before you cook the batter). Use a whisk to beat the batter until thick and smooth, then strain into a jug. This makes it easier to judge and control the amount you are pouring into the pan. Leave the batter to stand, preferably somewhere cool, for at least half an hour before using.

The ideal pan in which to make your pancake is a small, heavy-based omelette pan, although any frying pan will do. Heat the minimum amount of oil until a faint haze rises, then pour in a paper-thin covering of batter, tilting the pan to spread it evenly. If your batter is so thick that this is difficult, adjust the consistency by adding a little water or milk, and beating thoroughly. Cook the pancake on a steady heat for just two minutes, shaking the pan occasionally to prevent sticking. Then toss, or flip the pancake over with a palette knife, and cook the other side for a minute. If it is sticking and/or breaking up, don't worry – the temperature of the oil was probably not hot enough. Add a tiny drop more and heat it, then try again with a little more batter – you'll soon get the knack.

When making a number of pancakes to be served at the same time, keep them warm either by piling on a plate over a saucepan of boiling water, and covering with another plate, or by putting them into a barely warmed oven. You can also make them a few days before needed and keep them in a plastic box in the fridge, or store them for up to three months in the freezer.

There are a variety of ways in which you can serve your pancakes and *crêpes*. If they are thin, you can fold them around the filling, and top with a sauce, spoonful of cream or yogurt, sprinkling of nuts or fried crumbs. Crushed biscuits or crunchy oat cereal can be used with sweet *crêpes*. For special occasions, fit a number of folded *crêpes* into a heatproof dish, add sauce and/or topping, and grill or put into the oven for 10 minutes.

Another rather special way to serve them is to make a cake. Cook four or five pancakes and pile them up, spread flat, on top of each other. Between each pancake add a filling. A sweet cake could be sandwiched with cream whipped with yogurt, or nut cream, or tofu blended with honey, then with raw sugar jam or fruit *purée* or fresh fruit chopped or sliced, with a crunchy nut topping. A savoury cake made with ricotta or curd cheese mixed with finely chopped celery, sunflower seeds, and with a herb and tomato sauce over the top would be a winner with everyone. Cut your pancake cake into wedges to serve, possibly with extra sauce passed round in a jug.

PANCAKE BATTERS

Note: All quantities given here will make 8-10 small pancakes, depending on the thickness of the batter.

BATTER WITH EGG

4 oz (100g) plain wholemeal flour
1 egg
½ pt (275 ml) milk, or half milk and half water
Pinch of sea salt

1. Sieve together the flour and salt, then add the egg and stir briefly.

2. Gradually pour in the liquid, stirring continually to blend in the flour and remove lumps.

3. Beat energetically until you have a smooth, creamy batter.

4. Leave in the fridge for at least half an hour, then beat again before using.

BATTER WITH SOYA FLOUR (VEGAN)

4 oz (100g) plain wholemeal flour
2 oz (50g) soya flour
1 teaspoonful baking powder
½ pt (275 ml) water
Pinch of sea salt

1. Sieve together the flours, baking powder and salt.

2. Gradually stir in the water, then beat for a few minutes.

3. Leave in the fridge for at least half an hour, then beat again
    before using.

EXTRA RICH BATTER

4 oz (100g) plain wholemeal flour
2 large eggs
½ pt (275 ml) milk
Pinch of sea salt

Follow the method given for 'Batter with Egg'.

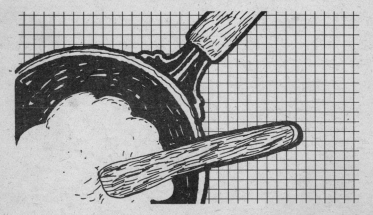

SOUFFLÉ BATTER
(for a lighter pancake)

4 oz (100g) plain wholemeal flour
2 eggs, separated
½ pt (275 ml) milk
Pinch of sea salt

1. Sieve the flour and salt together, then add the egg yolks, and stir lightly.

2. Gradually add the milk, stirring carefully, then beat well.

3. In another bowl, whisk the egg whites until just becoming stiff, then fold them into the batter.

4. Cook pancakes immediately.

BUCKWHEAT BATTER

3 oz (75g) buckwheat flour
2 oz (50g) plain wholemeal flour
1 egg
½ pt (275 ml) water
Pinch of sea salt

Sieve together the buckwheat and wholemeal flours, then follow the method given for 'Batter with Egg'.

YOGURT BATTER

4 oz (100 g) plain wholemeal flour
2 small cartons plain yogurt
1 large egg
Pinch of sea salt

1.   Sieve the flour and salt together, then combine with the yogurt. Mix well.

2.   Beat the egg to a froth then stir into the other ingredients.

3.   Leave in the fridge for at least half an hour, then beat again before using.

4.   As these pancakes are quite thick, they should be cooked over a gentle heat for longer than usual. Check that they are cooked through before serving.

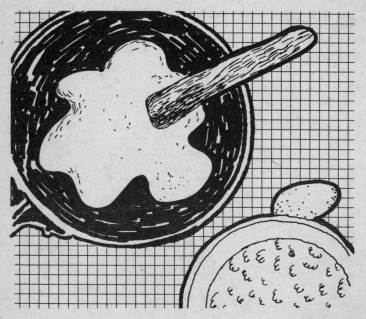

BATTER WITH OATMEAL

4 oz (100g) oatmeal
1 oz (25g) plain wholemeal flour
1 teaspoonful baking powder
1 small egg
Approx. ⅓ pt (200 ml) milk
1 teaspoonful vegetable oil
Pinch of sea salt

1. Sift together the flour, baking powder and salt; stir in the oatmeal and combine thoroughly.

2. Add the milk, oil and lightly beaten egg, and beat the mixture for a few minutes.

3. Leave to stand for an hour if possible; beat again; if too thick, adjust liquid with a little more milk.

4. Cook the minimum amount of batter at a time, using a steady heat; this is a heavier-textured pancake, and probably best served flat.

CORN BATTER

3 oz (75 g) cornmeal
2 oz (50 g) plain wholemeal flour
1 small egg
¼ pt (150 ml) milk
1 tablespoonful vegetable oil
Pinch of sea salt

1. Mix together the corn and wholemeal flours; season.

2. In another bowl, combine the lightly beaten egg, milk and oil; then add to the flour and beat well.

3. Leave to stand for at least half an hour, then beat again before using, and adjust the liquid if necessary.

Note: Maizemeal can be used instead of cornmeal, and as it is a lighter, finer flour, the results will be less heavy.

SAVOURY FILLINGS

POLISH BEETROOT PANCAKES

Pancake batter of your choice
1lb (450g) cooked beetroot
1 small carton soured cream
½-1 teaspoonful caraway seeds
Seasoning to taste

1. Cook pancakes; keep warm whilst preparing the filling.

2. Dice the beetroot and put into a small pan with the sour cream; heat gently for a few minutes.

3. Season the beetroot; add caraway seeds; divide mixture between the pancakes.

4. Serve with extra soured cream.

Note: If you do not like caraway seeds, leave them out and add instead a teaspoonful of chopped dill, or your favourite herbs.

BRUSSELS SPROUTS CREOLE PANCAKES

Pancake batter of your choice
1 lb (450g) small brussels sprouts
2 oz (50g) polyunsaturated margarine
1 medium onion
1 small pepper
1 clove of garlic, crushed
4 medium tomatoes
1 teaspoonful mixed herbs
Seasoning to taste

1. Cook pancakes and set aside.

2. Melt the margarine, then lightly *sauté* the sliced onion and pepper with the garlic.

3. Add the halved brussels sprouts, herbs and seasoning; cover pan and simmer for 10 minutes.

4. Chop the tomatoes, add to pan, and cook just long enough to heat through, then use vegetable mixture to fill the pancakes.

CURD CHEESE AND ONION PANCAKES

Pancake batter of your choice
4 oz (100g) curd cheese
Approx. 2 tablespoonsful milk
2 medium onions
1 tablespoonful vegetable oil
Seasoning to taste

1. Prepare and set aside pancakes.

2. Heat the oil and fry the sliced onions until crisp and golden brown; drain well.

3. Mash the curd cheese with the milk to make a creamy consistency, then stir in the onions and seasoning.

4. Fill pancakes with the cheese mixture.

SWEET CORN PANCAKES

Pancake batter of your choice
8 oz (225 g) sweet corn, fresh or frozen
1 small green pepper
1 small red pepper
½ small carton cream cheese, combined with the same amount of plain yogurt
Seasoning to taste
3 medium tomatoes

1. Prepare pancakes and keep warm.

2. Cook the sweet corn with the finely chopped peppers. Drain well.

3. Mix in the cheese and yogurt until it melts to make a sauce, then season to taste.

4. Use to fill pancakes, then top each one with a few slices of tomato.

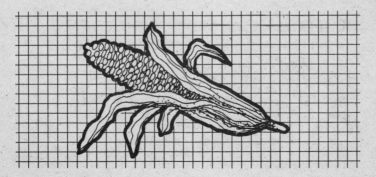

MUSHROOM PANCAKES WITH 'HOLLANDAISE SAUCE'

Pancake batter of your choice
8 oz (225 g) fresh mushrooms
1 tablespoonful vegetable oil
2 oz (50 g) polyunsaturated margarine
1 oz (25 g) plain wholemeal flour
½ pt (275 ml) milk
1 small egg yolk
A squeeze of lemon juice
Tarragon
Seasoning to taste

1. Make up pancakes and set aside.

2. Heat the oil and lightly *sauté* the sliced mushrooms, then drain on a paper towel.

3. Melt 1 oz (25 g) of the margarine in a pan and add the flour; *sauté* a few minutes then pour on the milk and bring to the boil, stirring continually.

4. When sauce thickens, remove from heat and let cool for a few minutes.

5. Beat rest of margarine, egg yolk, lemon juice and seasoning into the sauce.

6. Fill pancakes with mushrooms, fold, and serve sauce over the pancakes sprinkled with tarragon.

CELERY AND WALNUT PANCAKES

Pancake batter of your choice
1 head of celery
4 oz (100 g) walnut pieces
1 oz (25 g) polyunsaturated margarine
1 oz (25 g) plain wholemeal flour
½ pt (275 ml) milk or celery stock and 2 tablespoonsful
  skimmed milk powder
Seasoning to taste

1. Prepare pancakes and keep them warm whilst making the filling.

2. Chop the cleaned celery and steam until tender.

3. Make a sauce by melting the margarine in a pan, and stirring in the flour until it begins to brown. Add the milk, bring to the boil, still stirring, and simmer to make a thick white sauce.

4. Season the sauce, add the drained celery and walnut pieces.

5. Stuff the pancakes with the mixture, reserving a little of the sauce to pour on top. Alternatively, sprinkle with more chopped walnuts.

SUCCOTASH PANCAKES

Pancake batter of your choice
6 oz (175 g) broad beans or peas
6 oz (175 g) sweet corn
2 oz (50 g) polyunsaturated margarine
Parsley
Seasoning to taste

1. Make up the pancakes in the usual way.

2. Cook the beans or peas and sweet corn in the minimum of water until just tender, then drain.

3. Mix the margarine into the vegetables, season and add chopped parsley.

4. Fill pancakes with mixture and serve piping hot. Grated cheese on top goes well with the succotash filling.

CURRIED PANCAKES WITH CUCUMBER RAITA

Pancake batter of your choice
Approx. 2 teaspoonsful curry powder
1/3 pt (200 ml) plain yogurt
1 large cucumber
2 tablespoonsful chopped mint
Pinch of ground cumin seeds

1. When making the pancake batter, add curry powder to taste.

2. Cook and set aside the pancakes.

3. Beat the yogurt, then stir in the finely grated cucumber, seasoning and mint.

4. Use the mixture to fill the pancakes, or pour it over folded pancakes. Sprinkle with ground cumin.

SPINACH AND APPLE PANCAKES

Pancake batter of your choice
1 lb (450g) fresh or frozen spinach
1 medium apple
2 medium spring onions
Lemon juice
Seasoning to taste

1. Cook the pancakes and keep them warm.

2. In the minimum of water, cook the spinach until just tender, then chop finely.

3. Add the grated or finely sliced apple, chopped onions, juice and seasoning. Combine thoroughly.

4. Fill the prepared pancakes with the mixture. Yogurt or sieved cottage cheese go well with this recipe (or a mixture of the two).

SAUERKRAUT PANCAKES

Pancake batter of your choice
1 lb (450g) *Sauerkraut* (bought loose or home-made)
2 tablespoonsful seedless raisins
1 small carton plain yogurt
Seasoning to taste

1. Prepare and set aside pancakes.

2. Gently heat the *Sauerkraut* together with the raisins, stirring frequently.

3. Season well, then put a portion of the *Sauerkraut* onto each pancake, fold, and top with yogurt or sour cream.

Note: Sauerkraut can be flavoured various other ways too – try it with caraway seeds, finely chopped onion, carrot or apple slices, etc.

PANCAKES WITH BUTTER BEANS

Pancake batter of your choice
8 oz (225g) cooked butter beans
4 large ripe tomatoes
2 celery sticks
1 large onion
2 teaspoonsful oregano
1 tablespoonful vegetable oil
Parsley to garnish
Seasoning to taste

1. Cook the pancakes and keep them warm.

2. *Sauté* the sliced onion for a few minutes in the oil.

3. Add the finely chopped tomatoes and celery, herbs and seasoning, and cook a few minutes more.

4. Drain the beans and heat through in the sauce.

5. Either fill the pancakes with the mixture and garnish with fresh parsley; or, drain off most of the sauce, use the beans as a filling, and pour the sauce over the top of the folded pancakes.

EGG PANCAKES PROVENÇALE

Buckwheat batter, or another of your choice
4 eggs
1 medium aubergine
1 medium green pepper
2 medium tomatoes
2 oz (50 g) polyunsaturated margarine
4 oz (100 g) Cheddar cheese
Seasoning to taste

1. Prepare pancakes and set aside in a warm place.

2. Dice the aubergine, pepper and tomatoes, and *sauté* gently in the melted margarine until just tender. Season well.

3. Pour in the beaten eggs and cook for a few minutes, stirring from the bottom.

4. When the eggs start to set, remove from heat and use mixture to fill pancakes.

5. Fold pancakes, place neatly alongside each other in a shallow heat proof dish, sprinkle with grated cheese and grill briefly until cheese melts. Serve at once.

CHINESE-STYLE PANCAKES

Pancake batter of your choice
4 oz (100g) bean sprouts
4 sticks of celery
Small bunch of watercress
4 oz (100g) mushrooms
2 tablespoonsful vegetable oil
1 oz (25g) plain wholemeal flour
Pinch of raw cane sugar
Soy sauce
2 oz (50g) roasted peanuts
Seasoning to taste

1. Prepare pancakes and set aside.

2. Wash, dry, and remove stems from the watercress; wash and slice mushrooms; diagonally slice celery as thinly as possible.

3. Heat the oil and stir-fry these vegetables for just a few minutes.

4. In a cup, mix a little water with the flour, sugar and soy sauce, then pour over the vegetables and bring to boil.

5. Add bean sprouts, turn heat low, cover and simmer for a few minutes more.

6. Put a spoonful or two of the vegetables and sauce on each pancake, fold, and top with some chopped nuts.

SLIMMERS' PANCAKES

Pancake batter of your choice
8 oz (225 g) cottage cheese
1 small cucumber
Chopped chives to garnish
1/3 pt (200 ml) tomato juice
Seasoning to taste

1. Cook pancakes and leave in a warm place.

2. Mix together the cottage cheese, chopped cucumber, most of the chives, and seasoning.

3. Fill the pancakes with the cheese mixture, fold.

4. Heat the tomato juice gently and spread a little over each pancake, then sprinkle with the rest of the chopped chives.

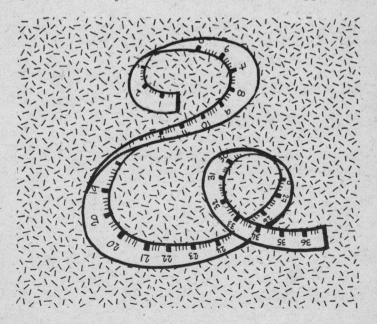

ALMOND CARROT PANCAKES

Pancake batter of your choice
8 oz (225 g) young carrots
1 oz (25 g) demerara raw cane sugar
1 oz (25 g) polyunsaturated margarine
1 tablespoonful finely grated orange peel
4 oz (100 g) chopped blanched almonds
Seasoning to taste

1. Prepare pancakes and set aside.

2. Gently melt the margarine in a pan, add the sugar, nuts, orange peel and seasoning. Cook for 5 minutes, stirring occasionally.

3. Slice the carrots very finely and simmer for 5-10 minutes in the almond sauce.

4. Fill each pancake with a portion of the vegetable mixture. More finely grated orange rind makes an attractive garnish.

PANCAKES WITH CHICK PEAS

Pancake batter of your choice
8 oz (225 g) cooked chick peas
4 tablespoonsful cream
2 oz (50 g) polyunsaturated margarine
Seasoning to taste
Chives to garnish

1. Prepare and set aside the pancakes.

2. Grind most of the chick peas to a paste, then stir in the margarine until it melts.

3. Add the cream and seasoning.

4. Fill each pancake with some of the chick pea sauce, then fold and top them with the rest of the peas cut up coarsely, and the chopped chives.

POTATO PANCAKES

4 large potatoes
2 oz (50g) plain wholemeal flour
2 oz (50g) grated Parmesan cheese
2 medium onions
4 oz (100g) cooked peas – optional
1 egg
1 teaspoonful garam masala
1 teaspoonful ground coriander
Seasoning to taste

1. Grate the peeled, raw potatoes; drain off surplus liquid.

2. Add to the finely chopped onion, flour, cheese, seasoning and drained peas.

3. Beat the egg, stir into the mixture. Season and add spices.

4. Drop by the spoonful into very hot fat, press lightly to make into a thin pancake, and cook until golden. Serve at once. This tastes particularly good with yogurt.

CREAMED ONION PANCAKES

Pancake batter of your choice
1 lb (450g) onions
2 tablespoonsful smooth peanut butter
A squeeze of lemon juice
Pinch of garlic
Soy sauce
1-2 oz (25-50g) roasted peanuts
Parsley to garnish
Sea salt and freshly ground black pepper

1. Prepare pancakes; set aside in a warm place.

2. Peel and coarsely slice onions, then cook in the minimum amount of water for 5-10 minutes, or until soft.

3. Stir in the peanut butter, add lemon juice, garlic, and a good sprinkling of soy sauce. Heat through.

4. Use the creamy onion mixture to fill the pancakes, then sprinkle with the chopped parsley, and a few nuts.

Note: To make this filling even creamier, stir in a spoonful or two of ricotta cheese; or, put a little on top of each pancake mixed with the nuts and chives.

CHEESY LEEKS PANCAKES

Pancake batter of your choice
1lb (450g) leeks
1oz (25g) polyunsaturated margarine
1oz (25g) plain wholemeal flour
½pt (275ml) milk
4oz (100g) cottage or *Quark* cheese
2oz (50g) Cheddar cheese
Pinch of paprika
Seasoning to taste

1. Make up pancakes and keep them warm.

2. Clean, chop and steam the leeks, or cook in the minimum of water.

3. Meanwhile, make a white sauce; heat the margarine until melted, stir in the flour and then the milk, and continue stirring until the sauce thickens.

4. Sieve or mash the cottage cheese and mix into the sauce with the drained leeks.

5. Stuff the pancakes with the mixture, fold, and place neatly in a heatproof dish. Sprinkle with the grated Cheddar and pop under the grill for one minute.

PANCAKES WITH SWEET AND SOUR CABBAGE

Pancake batter of your choice
1 small white cabbage
1 small onion
A few pineapple chunks (fresh or tinned in natural juice)
1 tablespoonful honey
2 tablespoonsful cider vinegar
2 oz (50 g) walnuts
Seasoning to taste

1. Make up pancakes and set aside in a wam place.

2. Shred the cabbage and put in pan with either a little water or pineapple juice mixed with the honey and vinegar.

3. Add finely chopped onion, cover and simmer until cooked.

4. Drain vegetables (reserving liquid), season, and mix with the pineapple chunks and chopped nuts.

5. Use mixture to fill pancakes. Pour the juice over the folded pancakes if liked.

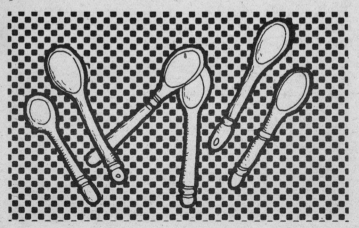

PARSNIP PANCAKES

Pancake batter of your choice
1lb (450g) fresh parsnips
1 small onion
1oz (25g) polyunsaturated margarine
1oz (25g) plain wholemeal flour
½pt (275ml) milk
Pinch of nutmeg
Seasoning to taste
Fresh parsley to garnish

1. Make up the pancakes and keep them warm.

2. Peel and cube the parsnips; steam until tender; drain.

3. Melt the margarine and lightly fry the sliced onion.

4. Sprinkle the flour onto the onion, stir, and cook for a few minutes, then remove pan from heat.

5. Pour on the milk, return to heat, and cook to make a bechamel sauce, stirring continually.

6. Blend with the parsnip cubes, add nutmeg and seasoning.

7. Fill pancakes with the parsnip mixture and garnish generously with the chopped parsley.

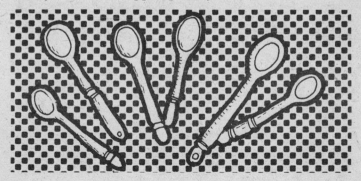

PANCAKES WITH SCRAMBLED EGGS

Pancake batter of your choice
4 eggs
4 tablespoonsful milk or cream
2 oz (50g) polyunsaturated margarine
4 oz (100g) mushrooms
Fresh chives to garnish
Seasoning to taste

1. Make up the pancakes and set aside to keep warm.

2. Beat together the eggs and milk, seasoning well; clean and slice the mushrooms.

3. Heat the margarine in a pan until it melts, then gently cook the mushroom slices for a few minutes, turning frequently.

4. Add the beaten eggs to the pan and stir slowly over a low heat until beginning to set; remove pan from heat.

5. Fill each pancake with some of the egg and mushroom mixture; fold and sprinkle with chopped chives.

VEGETABLE PANCAKE PIE

Pancake batter to make about 8 pancakes
8 oz (225g) carrots
½ pt (275 ml) white sauce
3 oz (75g) walnuts
1 oz (25g) polyunsaturated margarine
1 large cucumber
Parsley
Seasoning to taste

1. Peel, slice and steam the carrots until just tender.

2. Heat the margarine and gently *sauté* the walnuts for a few minutes.

3. Make the white sauce, add plenty of chopped parsley, drained carrots and seasoning.

4. Make up the pancakes in the usual way.

5. Put two pancakes on a baking sheet; spread generously with the cucumber slices; top each one with another pancake; top with walnuts; add another pancake and spoon on the carrots and sauce generously.

6. Top the two 'pies' with the last pancakes; decorate with more parsley and/or extra white sauce.

7. These can be served immediately cut into generous wedges, or put in the oven at 375°F/190°C (Gas Mark 5) for 10 minutes to warm through.

Note: Pancake pies can be made with any fillings, both hot and cold. (Try a cold version with salad ingredients and mayonnaise to add a creamy contrast to the crispness of the pancakes and fillings.) They can also be garnished as you like, with nuts, tomato slices or lightly fried mushrooms; and sauces can be added to the fillings or just poured over the top, maybe with some grated cheese sprinkled on finally to give a golden finish. Such pies can also, of course, be used with sweet ingredients.

CAULIFLOWER CHEESE PANCAKES

Pancake batter of your choice
1 medium cauliflower
4 cooking tomatoes
1 onion
2 tablespoonsful vegetable oil
2 tablespoonsful wholemeal breadcrumbs
1 oz (25 g) polyunsaturated margarine
1 teaspoonful mixed herbs
4 oz (100 g) cream or curd cheese

1. Melt the margarine in a saucepan; add the breadcrumbs and herbs; *sauté* until crumbs are crisp and golden. Set aside.

2. Trim and wash the cauliflower, divide into florets, steam until almost tender.

3. In another pan, heat the oil and add the sliced onion; cook gently until beginning to brown, then add the coarsely chopped tomatoes and cauliflower florets; season well, cover, and simmer.

4. Make the pancakes in the usual way.

5. Mix the cream cheese with a tiny amount of hot water to make a thick sauce.

6. Fill each pancake with some of the vegetable mixture; fold and arrange neatly in an ovenproof dish.

7. Pour the sauce over the pancakes, sprinkle with the breadcrumbs, and put the dish under a hot grill for a few minutes before serving.

LENTIL PANCAKES

Pancake batter of your choice
4 oz (100g) small red lentils
2 sticks celery
1 onion
1 teaspoonful rosemary
1 tablespoonful tomato *purée*
1 tablespoonful vegetable oil
Parsley to garnish
2 oz (50g) cooked rice or other grain – bulgur or millet for
    example
Seasoning to taste
Plain yogurt to serve

1. Heat the oil in a pan and *sauté* the finely chopped celery and
   onion for 5 minutes.

2. Add the lentils, rosemary, tomato *purée* and seasoning with
   just enough water to cover; bring to the boil, then simmer
   until the lentils form a thick *purée* (you may need to add more
   water during cooking).

3. Add the cooked, drained rice and blend well; cook for a few
   minutes longer.

4. Make the pancakes and fill each one with some of the lentil
   and rice mixture; serve with plain yogurt spooned over the
   top. (If you prefer you can mix the yogurt in with the
   lentils.) Garnish with parsley.

PEA AND CASHEW PANCAKES

Pancake batter of your choice
8 oz (225g) cooked green peas
4 oz (100g) cashew pieces
2 oz (50g) polyunsaturated margarine
1 tablespoonful vegetable oil
1 onion
½ clove garlic, crushed
1 oz (25g) plain wholemeal flour
¾ pt (425 ml) water
½ teaspoonful yeast extract, or to taste
Seasoning to taste
2 tablespoonsful plain yogurt or cream – optional

1. Heat the oil and lightly fry the garlic and finely chopped onion for 5-10 minutes.

2. Add the flour and cook briefly before pouring in the water, bringing to the boil, then simmering to make a sauce.

3. Season and add yeast extract to taste.

4. In a separate pan, melt the margarine and gently *sauté* the very finely chopped or ground cashew nuts until just beginning to brown; combine with the sauce and simmer for 5 minutes.

5. Add the drained peas and simmer for just a little longer.

6. Make the pancakes and fill each one with some of the mixture (into which you have stirred the yogurt, if desired). Fold and serve immediately.

COURGETTE PANCAKES
(All-in-one)

3 medium courgettes
1 large onion
2 oz (50 g) cooked sweet corn
2 oz (50 g) polyunsaturated margarine
2 tablespoonsful vegetable oil
½ pt (275 ml) milk and water
4 oz (100 g) plain wholemeal flour
1 egg
Seasoning to taste
1 small carton cream or curd cheese

1. Top and tail the courgettes; peel and slice the onion; coarsely grate the courgettes and *sauté* with the onion in the oil and melted margarine.

2. In a bowl, combine the flour and seasoning; gradually add the liquid and then the beaten egg; combine thoroughly.

3. Beat the mixture then leave to stand for a while; stir in the vegetables.

4. In a large frying pan, heat enough oil to give a thin coating; spoon in some of the batter and vegetables; tip the pan to spread the mixture evenly.

5. Cook gently until beginning to brown underneath; flip pancake or turn with a spatula and cook other side until set.

6. Keep pancake warm whilst using up the rest of the mixture in the same way.

7. Serve one or two per person and top each pancake with some cheese so that it melts to make a creamy sauce.

RED CABBAGE PANCAKES

Pancake batter of your choice
1 medium red cabbage
1 medium onion
1 large cooking apple
1 tablespoonful vegetable oil
Approx. ¼ pt (150 ml) vegetable stock or water
2 tablespoonsful cider vinegar
1 tablespoonful raw cane sugar or honey
2 teaspoonsful caraway seeds, or to taste
Seasoning to taste

1. Heat the oil and *sauté* the sliced onion for a few minutes; add the finely chopped cabbage and cook for 5 minutes more, stirring occasionally.

2. Stir together the stock, cider vinegar and sweetener, and add to the pan with the peeled and sliced apple; cover and cook gently until the cabbage is almost cooked, but not too soft.

3. Add seasoning and seeds, cook a few minutes longer.

4. Meanwhile make the pancakes and when they are ready, fill each one with some of the cabbage mixture, fold and serve.

Note: Delicious as this may be, it is not very rich in protein. You can solve this problem by using an extra rich batter that includes eggs and milk, or add some nuts to the cabbage and/or serve with sour cream into which some finely grated cheese has been stirred. Yogurt also goes well with red cabbage cooked this way.

BAKED PANCAKES

Pancake batter of your choice
5 oz (150g) ham-flavoured soya 'meat' chunks, hydrated
1 large onion
1-2 tablespoonsful vegetable oil
2 eggs
½ pt (275 ml) milk
1 teaspoonful plain wholemeal flour
3 oz (75g) Cheddar cheese
Seasoning to taste
Good pinch of paprika

1. Make up the pancakes and set aside.

2. Heat the oil and lightly *sauté* the sliced onion for a few minutes; add the drained soya meat chunks and *sauté* with the onion, turning frequently.

3. Add the minimum amount of water and continue cooking for 10 minutes; or until the soya meat is cooked.

4. Grease an ovenproof dish; fill each pancake with some of the onion mixture; fold and arrange side by side in the dish.

5. In a separate bowl beat together the eggs, milk and flour; season well, then pour over the pancakes; sprinkle with grated cheese.

6. Bake at 375°F/190°C (Gas Mark 5) for 20-30 minutes, or until the egg custard is set. Sprinkle with paprika and serve piping hot.

SUMMER PANCAKES

Pancake batter of your choice
1 crisp lettuce
12 radishes
4 large firm tomatoes
1 cucumber
6 spring onions

For Dressing
½ pt (275 ml) mayonnaise
¼ pt (150 ml) plain yogurt
A squeeze of lemon juice
Seasoning to taste

1. Make the pancakes as thin as possible; set aside to cool completely.

2. Wash and prepare the salad ingredients in the usual way; combine them in a bowl; stir in seasoning to taste.

3. Blend the mayonnaise, yogurt, lemon juice and seasoning together well; chill briefly.

4. Stir a little of the dressing in with the salad ingredients; distribute them between the pancakes and fold up.

5. Serve the salad pancakes with more dressing spooned over the top.

Note: Obviously any and every kind of salad ingredient can be used in these pancakes, including finely chopped vegetables such as cauliflower. Nuts or seeds can be added if you wish; also grated cheese. The dressing can also be varied to suit your particular preference, but try to include something containing protein. Nut butter can be made more liquid, and poured over the pancakes – left-over hummus is delicious.

MARROW GALETTES

Buckwheat batter
1 small marrow
1 large onion
6 tomatoes
3 tablespoonsful tomato *purée*
4 oz (100g) cooked peas or beans
1 generous teaspoonful mixed herbs
2 oz (50g) grated Parmesan cheese
1-2 tablespoonsful vegetable oil
Parsley to garnish
Seasoning to taste

1. Heat the oil in a large pan and add the sliced onion; cook gently for a few minutes.

2. Add the chopped tomatoes, herbs, seasoning and tomato *purée*; cook gently for 5 more minutes.

3. Peel and cube the marrow (discard the seeds) and add to the pan; mix well; cover the pan and simmer until the marrow is tender.

4. Make up the pancakes.

5. Add the drained peas or beans to the vegetables, stir well, and use this mixture to fill the pancakes.

6. Fold, and serve sprinkled generously with the grated cheese and garnished with the chopped parsley.

Note: Galettes are traditionally made with buckwheat flour. If you cannot obtain it, but *can* buy buckwheat, you can grind this (a small coffee grinder will do the job) and use the resulting flour for a finer, whiter-looking *galette*.

CHESTNUT AND ONION PANCAKES

Pancake batter of your choice
1 lb (450g) chestnuts
2 large onions
2 oz (50g) polyunsaturated margarine
1 teaspoonful mixed herbs – optional
Seasoning to taste

1. Slit the chestnuts and cook them in boiling water for 10 minutes; then remove shell and inner skin.

2. Boil again, then reduce water temperature and simmer chestnuts for 15-30 minutes, or until just tender.

3. Melt the margarine and gently *sauté* the sliced onion with the herbs; when beginning to colour, add the whole chestnuts (if you prefer you can chop them coarsely). Continue frying, turning frequently.

4. Make up the pancakes and fold each one around a portion of the chestnut and onion mixture; trickle some of the fat in which they cooked over them.

Note: Chopped mushrooms can also be fried with the nuts and onions; the herbs can be varied; a little cream or soured cream could be stirred into the mixture just before it is added to the pancakes.

PANCAKES WITH A DIFFERENCE

WAFFLES

These are made with a mixture similar to that used for pancakes, but are cooked in a special waffle iron to produce a crisp biscuit-like base on which you can serve savoury or sweet toppings.

CHEESE WAFFLES

8 oz (225 g) plain wholemeal flour
½ pt (275 ml) milk
2 eggs
4 oz (100 g) polyunsaturated margarine
6 oz (175 g) Cheddar cheese
1 teaspoonful herbs

1. Soften the margarine, put it into a bowl with the flour, milk, eggs, and herbs; blend very thoroughly.

2. The mixture should be thick and creamy; add more milk or water if it is too dry.

3. Finely grate the cheese and stir it into the rest of the ingredients.

4. Heat and oil the waffle iron; pour in the batter to fill two-thirds of the iron; close firmly and cook in the usual way.

SOYA WAFFLES

8 oz (225 g) soya flour, sifted
2 teaspoonsful baking powder
2 oz (50 g) polyunsaturated margarine
2 oz (50 g) light muscovado raw cane sugar
3 eggs
½ pt (275 ml) milk

1. In a bowl combine the softened margarine with all the remaining ingredients; then beat thoroughly to lighten the mixture.

2. If too thick, add more milk or water to the batter.

3. Heat and oil the waffle iron; pour in the batter to fill two-thirds of the iron; close firmly and cook in the usual way. Serve simply with maple syrup or honey; or top with sliced bananas or any other fruit; apple sauce also goes well with this.

PEANUT WAFFLES

4 oz (100g) plain wholemeal flour
2 teaspoonsful baking powder
3 tablespoonsful honey
2 eggs
4 oz (100g) peanut butter
¾ pt (425 ml) milk
½ teaspoonful vanilla essence
Good pinch of sea salt

1. Combine the flour and baking powder in a bowl; stir in the salt.

2. In another bowl beat together the eggs, honey and vanilla; mix thoroughly with the peanut butter and milk.

3. Add the liquid to the dry ingredients, stir well.

4. Heat and oil the waffle iron; pour in batter to fill two-thirds of the iron; close firmly and cook in the usual way.

TORTILLAS

These flat, thin cornmeal pancakes are like daily bread to the Mexicans, where they can be used as a fork to scoop up food, as a dip for hot chilli sauces; can be folded and topped with savoury ingredients, or wrapped around them.

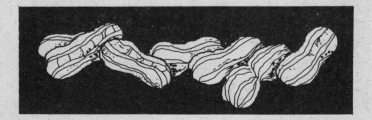

BASIC RECIPE

8 oz (225 g) cornmeal
Approx. ½ pt (275 ml) warm water
Sea salt to taste

1. Sift together the flour and salt; gradually stir in enough water to make a dough; knead briefly.

2. Divide into twelve portions and roll out on a floured surface to make them into 6 inch circles.

3. Cook the tortillas one at a time in a skillet or heavy-based pan; traditionally, you should not need any oil, but should just cook the tortillas over a medium heat for a few minutes on each side, until lightly browned. If you prefer, you can shallow fry them in a minimum amount of oil.

WHEAT AND CORNMEAL TORTILLAS

4 oz (100 g) cornmeal
4 oz (100 g) plain wholemeal flour
3 tablespoonsful vegetable oil
Barely ¼ pt (150 ml) warm water
Sea salt to taste
Vegetable oil for frying

1. Sieve together the cornmeal, flour and salt.

2. Add the oil and enough water to make a soft dough; knead for a few minutes; leave to stand for 15-30 minutes.

3. Divide into twelve portions and roll out, on a floured surface, to make them into 6 inch circles.

4. Heat the oil and gently fry the tortillas, one at a time, until cooked through, turning during the cooking to lightly brown both sides.

BEAN ENCHILADAS

12 cooked tortillas
Approx. 8 oz (225 g) cooked mixed beans (left-overs are ideal)

For Sauce
1 onion
½-1 clove garlic, crushed
2 tablespoonsful vegetable oil
4 ripe tomatoes
2 tablespoonsful tomato *purée*
½-1 tablespoonful chilli powder, or to taste
1 teaspoonful paprika
1 small carton soured cream
Seasoning to taste

1. Make up the tortillas and, whilst still warm, wrap each one around some of the bean mixture.

2. Arrange close together in a heatproof dish with the join facing downwards.

3. In a saucepan, heat the oil and lightly *sauté* the sliced onion with the garlic for 10 minutes; add the chopped tomatoes, *purée*, chilli powder, paprika and seasoning.

4. Bring the sauce to the boil, then lower the heat, cover and simmer until a thick paste is formed; adjust seasoning.

5. Pour sauce evenly over the tortillas; spoon the sour cream over the top; bake at 350°F/180°C (Gas Mark 4) for 10-15 minutes, or until heated through.

GRIDDLE CAKES

Originally cooked – as their name implies – on a hot griddle, these easy-to-make cakes or scones can also be made in a heavy-based frying pan. Thicker than pancakes, they need to be cooked slowly so that the inside is ready at the same time as the outside. As they are usually made in small 2 inch rounds, they are not folded, but served with a sweet or savoury topping or sauce poured over them.

WHEAT GERM GRIDDLE CAKES

3 oz (75g) plain wholemeal flour
2 tablespoonsful wheat germ
2 teaspoonsful baking powder
1/3 pt (200 ml) milk
1 egg
1 tablespoonful honey
Pinch of sea salt
1 tablespoonful vegetable oil

1. Sift together the flour, wheat germ, baking powder and salt.

2. Add the milk, honey, lightly beaten egg and oil; mix all the ingredients together thoroughly but lightly.

3. Lightly oil a heavy frying pan, heat, and pour a little of the batter into the pan; cook the griddle cake until beginning to brown then flip over and cook the other side. Serve warm or cold with margarine or butter, honey or raw sugar jam; or top with cream cheese and chives for an unusual combination; with peanut butter for a children's tea.

Note: This basic recipe can be adapted with the addition of finely chopped dried fruit or nuts or spices; alternatively, omit the sweetening and use herbs instead, maybe with some finely chopped courgettes or onion.

YOGURT GRIDDLE CAKES

1 small carton plain yogurt
1 oz (25 g) plain wholemeal flour
1-2 tablespoonsful vegetable oil
1 egg
Sea salt to taste

1. Sieve the flour; discard the bran (it can be used in another dish).

2. Beat the egg, then add to the yogurt; mix well, fold in the flour and a pinch of salt.

3. Heat the oil in a heavy pan and cook a little of the batter until just beginning to brown; turn and cook the other side; use the rest of the batter in the same way.

4. Serve whilst still warm with lemon juice and a generous sprinkling of raw cane sugar.

BLINIS

Blinis, also called blintzes, are traditional Jewish cheese pancakes, and should be made from buckwheat flour. However, they are in fact often made from wheat flour – and filled with a variety of ingredients, including caviar! Try this basic recipe, then adapt it to suit the items you have available – and those that your family like best! (These are the thinner version that can be rolled around a filling; blinis can also be made with yeast to produce a flat pancake that is too thick to fold, but is topped with whatever you choose instead.)

2 oz (50g) buckwheat flour
2 oz (50g) plain wholemeal flour
2 eggs
¼ pt (150 ml) milk
Pinch of sea salt
1 tablespoonful vegetable oil

For Filling
8 oz (225 g) cottage cheese, ricotta or cream cheese
2 oz (50g) powdered raw cane sugar, or to taste
Few drops vanilla essence or lemon juice

1. Sieve together the two flours and the salt.

2. Use a wooden spoon to beat the eggs and milk into the dry ingredients; combine thoroughly.

3. Heat the minimum amount of oil in a heavy-based pan (or simply brush with oil); pour in a little of the batter and make a pancake in the usual way.

4. Mash the cheese with the sugar and essence or juice; use the mixture to fill the pancakes; serve with raw sugar jam if liked.

Note: In fact, the accepted way to serve blinis is to fry them gently in a little butter *after they have been filled*. They need to be handled with care so that they do not fall apart, or lose their filling - cooking them this way does, of course, boost the fat involved, but for special occasions is well worth the extra effort. Dust with powdered sugar.

PITA

Greek pita bread is nothing like a pancake, but is included here because it can be used in a similar way – as a wrapping for savoury ingredients, that is. Particularly good with such dishes as falafels, (curried vegetables), and also with salad, it is easier to make than most people think.

8 oz (225 g) wholemeal flour
¼ oz (7 g) fresh yeast
½ teaspoonful raw cane sugar or honey
¼ pt (150 ml) warm water
Pinch of sea salt

1. Sieve together the flour and salt.

2. Stir the yeast and sugar into the warm water, mixing well until dissolved, then set aside for 15 minutes or so to froth up.

3. Pour into the flour mixture and knead to make a smooth dough; turn onto a lightly floured board and continue kneading until the dough is very elastic.

4. Leave the dough to rise, then knead again lightly; divide into eight portions and roll out to the traditional oval shape about ¼ inch thick.

5. Arrange on a greased baking sheet and cook at 400°F/200°C (Gas Mark 6) for about ten minutes, or until risen. Cool on a wire rack, then when needed, slit along the side to make a pocket and fill with the ingredients of your choice.

Note: These can also be cooked in a heavy-based pan; lightly grease the pan and put it over a strong heat; when ready, slip pitas one at a time into the pan and press down with a spatula as it cooks; flip over and cook the other side until just coloured.

SWEET-TOOTH CRÊPES

CRÊPES BELLE HÉLÈNE

Pancake batter of your choice
4 medium pears (conference are ideal)
2 oz (50 g) light muscovado raw cane sugar
A squeeze of lemon juice
1 teaspoonful grated lemon rind
1 small bar raw sugar chocolate
2 tablespoonsful milk or single cream
1 oz (25 g) flaked almonds

1. Peel, core and quarter the pears; put them in a saucepan, cover with water, add sugar, lemon juice and rind, and simmer gently until tender.

2. In a bowl, over a pan of water, melt the broken chocolate, stirring continually, and adding enough milk or cream to make a sauce-like consistency.

3. Make up the pancakes in the usual way; fill each one with a portion of the coarsely chopped pears and a little of the juice; fold and top with some sauce and a sprinkling of nuts.

Note: If you prefer, you can drain the pears thoroughly and serve the juice separately in a jug.

RASPBERRY CRÊPES

Pancake batter of your choice
1 lb (450g) fresh raspberries
3 oz (75g) demerara raw cane sugar, or to taste
¼ pt (150ml) plain yogurt
¼ pt (150ml) whipping cream

1. Wash and then drain the raspberries.

2. Whip together the cream and yogurt to make a kind of *'crème fraiche'*; chill briefly.

3. Make the pancakes, fill each one generously with fruit, sprinkle with sugar, and top with the yogurt cream.

CRÊPES WITH PINEAPPLE AND GINGER

Pancake batter of your choice
1 small pineapple or 1 tin of pineapple in natural juice
4 oz (100g) wholemeal ginger biscuits
A few pieces of stem ginger preserved in honey

1. Crush the pineapple flesh (not too fine or it will disintegrate) and moisten with some of the natural juice and/or a few spoonsful of the ginger-flavoured honey; mix in the finely chopped ginger.

2. Crumble the biscuits coarsely and mix half of them with the fruit.

3. Make up the pancakes in the usual way; fill each one with some of the fruit mixture; fold and sprinkle with the remaining ginger crumbs.

Note: You could also make a sauce by heating together 2 oz (50g) light muscovado raw cane sugar with about ½ pt (275 ml) of pineapple juice and ginger honey combined, and stirring until the sauce thickens. Serve over the pancakes and then sprinkle with crumbs, if desired.

CHRISTMAS CRÊPES

Pancake batter of your choice
8 oz (225 g) raw sugar mincemeat (see page 57)
2 oz (50 g) raw cane sugar
Orange butter*

1. Make pancakes and when ready to serve them, simply spread each one with butter and mincemeat, roll up, and dust with some powdered raw cane sugar.

*To make orange butter
3 oz (75 g) butter or polyunsaturated margarine
6 oz (175 g) raw cane sugar, powdered in grinder
2-3 tablespoonsful fresh orange juice
2 tablespoonsful finely grated orange rind

1. Cream together the fat and powdered sugar; beat in the juice and grated rind; leave to set before using.

Note: You can use lemon instead of orange or brandy if you wish to be really traditional.

BANANA WALNUT CRÊPES

Pancake batter of your choice
4 ripe bananas
1-2 tablespoonsful maple syrup or honey
A squeeze of lemon juice
2 oz (50 g) walnut pieces
1 oz (25 g) polyunsaturated margarine – optional

1. Mash the bananas to a smooth cream with the lemon juice and sweetener; gently sauté the walnut pieces in the melted fat.

2. Make up the pancakes and fill each one with the banana cream; fold and sprinkle with the buttered nuts before serving.

Note: As an alternative you can cut the bananas into chunks, toss in the combined juice and syrup, and mix with the raw coarsely chopped nuts. Use a little melted butter instead of a sauce to trickle over the top of your folded pancakes.

COTTAGE CHEESE CRÊPES

Pancake batter of your choice
1 small carton plain cottage cheese
2 oz (50g) raisins
2 oz (50g) demerara raw cane sugar
2 oz (50g) chopped roasted hazelnuts
Grated rind of a small lemon

1. Mix together the cottage cheese, raisins, sugar, nuts and lemon rind, and leave to stand for a while so that the flavours blend. (For a smoother mixture, *purée* the cottage cheese first.)

2. Make up the pancakes; use the cottage cheese to fill each one before folding, sprinkle with some extra sugar if desired. If you prefer, fill the pancakes with fresh chopped fruit and use the cottage cheese as a sauce to go over the top.

CRÊPES WITH LEMON CURD

Pancake batter of your choice
4 oz (100g) raw sugar lemon curd
A squeeze of lemon juice
1-2 oz (25-50g) demerara raw cane sugar
2 oranges – optional

1. Make up the pancakes in the usual way; spread with the lemon curd whilst still warm; sprinkle with juice; fold up.

2. Top with some sugar, and – if you like – a few slices of orange arranged attractively.

ALMOND CRUNCH CRÊPES

Pancake batter of your choice
2 oz (50g) polyunsaturated margarine
2 oz (50g) demerara raw cane sugar
2 oz (50g) blanched almonds
Vanilla ice cream

1. Make up the pancakes and keep warm.

2. Melt the margarine in a pan, add the sugar and chopped almonds, heat gently until the nuts begin to brown.

3. Just before serving, spoon some ice cream onto each pancake, fold immediately, and sprinkle with some of the almond crunch. Serve at once.

Note: An easier way to get a similar taste is to top your *crêpes* with coarsely crushed macaroons.

SPICY APPLE CRÊPES

Pancake batter of your choice
1½-2 lb (675-900g) cooking apples
2 tablespoonsful vegetable oil
4 oz (100g) raw cane sugar
2 oz (50g) raisins
1 teaspoonful cinnamon, or to taste

1. Make a *purée* of the apples by peeling and slicing them, then *sautéeing* gently in the oil for a few minutes before adding the sugar, raisins and spice to taste; cover and cook until soft.

2. Make the pancakes and fill with the hot apple *purée*; dust the folded pancakes with extra cinnamon. You could also sprinkle on more raisins.

PRUNE AND YOGURT CRÊPES

Pancake batter of your choice
8 oz (225g) prunes
1 small carton plain yogurt

1. Soak the prunes overnight, then simmer until very soft; mash them to make a thick *purée* (or use a blender).

2. Mix this well with the yogurt, then chill.

3. Make the pancakes as usual; fill with the *purée* and fold.

Note: These pancakes could be served with extra yogurt, or sprinkled with crunchy demerara raw cane sugar mixed with some lemon rind.

MARMALADE CRÊPES

Pancake batter of your choice
4 oz (100g) grapefruit, ginger or orange marmalade
¼ pt (150ml) single cream

1. Make up the pancakes, then spread each one right to the edge with the marmalade of your choice.

2. Roll up into a tight roll and serve with single cream.

Note: You could also, of course, top these with fruit or with crumbled biscuits; crunchy oat cereal also tastes good, especially with the sharper marmalades. Jams can be used in the same way. Marmalades and jams can also be mixed with the appropriate fruits to make a filling.

FRUIT AND NUT CREAM CRÊPES

Pancake batter of your choice
1 small melon
4 oz (100g) fresh strawberries
4 oz (100g) cashew nuts
1-2 teaspoonsful honey

1. Peel and chop the melon; wash and halve the strawberries; mix together with the juice from the melon, and a little honey if liked.

2. Grind the cashews to a fine powder, then add enough water to make into a cream; add honey if you want a sweeter cream.

3. Make up the pancakes; fill at once with the fruit mixture; fold and top with the nut cream.

CRÊPES AUX MARRONS

Pancake batter of your choice
12 oz (350g) chestnuts or 1 tin unsweetened chestnut *purée*
2 oz (50g) polyunsaturated margarine
2 oz (50g) raw cane sugar, powdered in grinder
Approx. ½ teaspoonful vanilla essence
2 large ripe peaches

1. Slit the ends of the chestnuts and boil in water until soft enough to mash, sieve or blend (this takes about 30 minutes, but depends on the size and freshness of the chestnuts).

2. Add the sugar and vanilla essence; stir in the margarine until it melts. Keep the sauce hot whilst making the pancakes.

3. Fold each cooked pancake around a few spoonsful of the chestnut sauce; decorate the top with slices of fresh peach. Alternatively, mix the fruit in with the chestnuts and use to fill the pancakes; serve sprinkled with a little vanilla sugar and/or whipped cream.

CREAM CHEESE CRÊPES WITH CHERRIES

Pancake batter of your choice
8 oz (225 g) cream or curd cheese
2 oz (50 g) demerara raw cane sugar
Milk to mix
8 oz (225 g) fresh or frozen black cherries

1. Mash the cheese to a thick cream; add a little milk if it is too thick; sweeten with sugar.

2. Make the pancakes in the usual way; fill each one with some of the cream; sprinkle with sugar; fold and top with cherries.

Note: Ricotta cheese makes a lighter yet still creamy filling, as does cottage cheese that has been mashed or sieved – the sweetening changes their character completely. Instead of just serving the fruit as it is, you can make a sauce with a little fruit juice and a teaspoonful of arrowroot; bring to the boil and simmer until it thickens, add the cherries for just a minute or two, and pour over the pancakes whilst still hot.

TAHINI HONEY CRÊPES

Pancake batter of your choice
Approx. 4 tablespoonsful light tahini
Approx. 2 tablespoonsful honey
3 oz (75 g) raisins or 2 apples
Grated orange rind

1. Make the pancakes in the usual way.

2. Mix the tahini with enough water to make a thick, smooth spread; sweeten with honey; cover each pancake with a thin layer of the mixture.

3. Sprinkle with raisins and finely grated rind; or use coarsely chopped apple instead (you could also combine all the ingredients!).

4. Roll up the pancakes and serve as they are, or sliced like a Swiss roll.

ORANGE AND APRICOT CRÊPES

Pancake batter of your choice
3 medium oranges
¼pt (150ml) fresh orange juice
3 tablespoonsful raw sugar apricot jam
Desiccated coconut

1. Make the pancakes and set aside to keep warm.

2. In a saucepan, combine the juice and apricot jam, and heat gently, stirring continually, to make a sauce.

3. Slice the peeled oranges as finely as possible, fill the pancakes with the fruit (you may need to moisten it with some more juice); sprinkle with coconut; fold the pancakes and cover with the sauce.

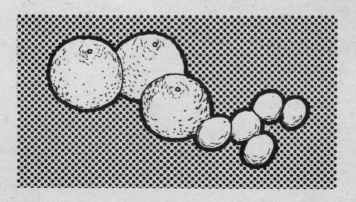

SIMPLE CRÊPES SUZETTE

Pancake batter of your choice
1 oz (25 g) polyunsaturated margarine
1 orange or lemon
2 oz (50 g) honey
Brandy or liqueur – optional

1. Make up the pancakes and, when four are ready, fold into quarters.

2. Melt the margarine in a large frying pan; add the juice of the orange or lemon and honey; stir well and continue cooking gently until bubbling hot; add liqueur, if using it.

3. Fit the four pancakes into the pan and simmer them in the sauce for a few minutes; serve with the sauce poured over them, and – if you like – some of the finely grated fruit rind.

4. Traditionally, brandy is warmed, set alight, and poured over the pancakes just before they are served.

ICE CREAM CRÊPES WITH MELBA SAUCE

Pancake batter of your choice
Vanilla ice cream

For Sauce
8 oz (225 g) fresh or frozen raspberries
2 oz (50 g) light muscovado raw cane sugar
Approx. $1/3$ pt (200 ml) water
2 teaspoonsful arrowroot

1. Wash the raspberries, then put them into a saucepan with nearly all of the water; mix the rest of it with the arrowroot then add to the fruit.

2. Bring to boil, then simmer until the sauce is thick; stir well then set aside to cool.

3. Make pancakes in the usual way; take ice cream straight from the freezer and slice; distribute slices between pancakes; roll up, and arrange neatly (and speedily) in a greased heatproof dish.

4. Heat pancakes through in a ready-warmed oven (at 425°F/220°C (Gas Mark 7) for 3 minutes only; serve with the melba sauce.

APRICOT NUT CRÊPES

Pancake batter of your choice
8 oz (225 g) dried apricots, soaked overnight
1 oz (25 g) sunflower seeds
1 oz (25 g) sesame seeds
1 oz (25 g) chopped walnuts
1-2 teaspoonsful mixed spice
A squeeze of lemon juice
1 tablespoonful honey
Approx. 1 teaspoonful arrowroot

1. Cook the dried apricots gently until soft enough to mash to a thick *purée* (although, if you prefer, you can leave them whole).

2. Mix the drained fruit with the seeds, walnuts, spice.

3. Use a little of the liquid in which the apricots were cooked to make a sauce: put most of it in a saucepan, add the lemon juice and honey, mix remaining juice with the arrowroot and add to the pan; boil, then simmer the sauce until thick.

4. Make the pancakes; fold each one around the fruit and nut mixture; top with the syrup. Yogurt tastes delicious with these *crêpes*.

CASHEW CRÊPES

Pancake batter of your choice
2 oz (50 g) finely chopped cashew nuts
2 oz (50 g) demerara raw cane sugar
1 tablespoonful rose-water or orange flower water, or to
   taste

1. When making up the batter for the pancakes, add the finely chopped nuts (they have a delicate flavour if left raw, but roasted nuts can be used too).

2. Then proceed to make the pancakes in the usual way.

3. Heat the sugar with a little water and rosewater to taste; simmer to make a syrup.

4. So that the syrup permeates the pancakes, it is best to arrange them folded in a heatproof dish; pour on the syrup; heat through in the oven for 5 to 10 minutes. A few cashews can be sprinkled on top.

CRÊPES WITH RICOTTA CHEESE

Pancake batter of your choice
4 oz (100 g) ricotta cheese
2 tablespoonsful whipped cream
1 oz (25 g) chopped dried peel
1 oz (25 g) *glacé* cherries
2 oz (50 g) roasted blanched almonds
2 oz (50 g) raw cane sugar, powdered in grinder

1. Combine the ricotta and whipped cream; stir in the chopped peel and cherries, coarsely chopped almonds and most of the sugar (or to taste).

2. Make the pancakes in the usual way; divide the creamy cheese mixture between them; dust with a little more sugar before serving. You could also decorate with more dried peel, cherries and nuts, if you wish.

Note: Make your candied peel and cherries at home, and you can be sure they contain only raw cane sugar, no preservatives or artificial colouring. You can substitute them in this recipe with freshly grated rind and raisins; the sweetness of the mixture might need to be adjusted.

LEMON SORBET CRÊPES

Pancake batter of your choice
Lemon sorbet

For Chocolate Sauce
2 tablespoonsful cocoa powder
4 tablespoonsful water
1 tablespoonful raw cane sugar
1 tablespoonful honey

1. Put all the ingredients for the chocolate sauce together into the top of a double boiler, or a heavy-based pan; heat very gently, stirring continually, until you have a thick sauce. Adjust sweetness if necessary.

2. Make the pancakes and fill each one with a portion of the sorbet.

3. Fold; top with the cooled sauce and serve immediately.

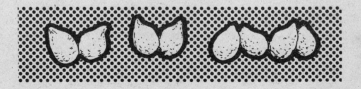

INDEX